Published in celebration of the 125th anniversary of the

founding of the University of Wisconsin–Madison

Harold M. Groves

TAX

PHILOSOPHERS

*Two Hundred Years
of Thought
in Great Britain and the
United States*

Edited by

Donald J. Curran

THE UNIVERSITY OF WISCONSIN PRESS

The publication of this book
has been made possible
with the assistance of the
Harold Groves Memorial Fund

Published 1974
The University of Wisconsin Press
Box 1379, Madison, Wisconsin 53701

The University of Wisconsin Press, Ltd.
70 Great Russell Street, London

First printing

Printed in the United States of America

For LC CIP information see the colophon

ISBN 0-299-06660-6

Contents

Editor's Preface

Harold Groves strongly influenced the world around him during the seventy-two years of his life. Although he died in December 1969, it is hoped that his influence may continue through this book.

Professor Groves started work on the book in the late 1950s but never submitted it for publication. During a 1971 visit with Mrs. Groves in Madison, I learned that nothing had been done about the manuscript since her husband's death. My own interest in it began in 1960, when I took his graduate course called "Philosophers and Philosophies of Taxation"; the interest grew over the years as a result of numerous conversations about philosophy in general and about this manuscript in particular. With the encouragement of Mrs. Groves, I was able to find all the pertinent materials in the twenty-six cartons containing drafts of all the chapters of the book, the author's class notes, and various other notes that fortunately offered many clues to guide the editorial work of preparing the manuscript for publication.

The volume represents a happy and rare combination of elements. A scholar respected as a leader in his field sat back after forty years of learning and doing to survey the Great Books (as he put it) of public finance. The background he brought to the survey included not only his long years of academic work at the University of Wisconsin but also the practical experience of his three terms in the Wisconsin Legislature, his service as state tax commissioner, his work with the federal government in Washington, and the fiscal studies he made for state and municipal governments.

A younger scholar, or a team of them, can put together a competent survey of public finance literature. Valuable as such a contribution surely is, it can hardly contain the judicious balance or the welcome spice found in Mr. Groves's work. He frequently inserted what he calls in the first chapter a "presentation (sometimes implicit) of a point of view of our own." In the editor's view, the book may well become a classic because of the wisdom, the balance, and the humanity manifested in these expressions of the author's point of view.

Harold Groves often expressed the conviction that there are relatively few central issues in taxation and that these few issues keep surfacing over time precisely because they do not allow of final solution. This conviction guided his selection of men and ideas in the chapters that follow. Thus, the volume is not intended to be comprehensive. It is hoped, however, that it will enrich others as we who knew and studied with Harold Groves have been enriched.

Harold M. Groves

TAX

PHILOSOPHERS

1

Introduction

This book is a series of essays on public finance literature that examines criti-
cally some of the Great Books in the field. It offers a classification of authors
according to their points of view and the presentation (sometimes implicit) of
a point of view of our own. In order to give the reader a setting for the authors
and their works, some attention is given to the history of tax institutions and
to biographical facts about authors. The book is selective rather than exhaus-
tive and makes no pretense of presenting a complete history of economic
thought, even as it applies to public finance. The concentration on authors
who published in English is conceded and regretted; it is accounted for in part
by the author's linguistic limitations. The emphasis is primarily on the philosophical rather than the economic aspects of taxation.

The major outline of the book follows an attempted division of authors
into four schools of thought; the last chapter of Part IV discusses Keynes and
taxation for aggregative goals. The first group, whom we may call the *rationalists,* gives primary weight to the distribution of taxes according to some measure of the economic capacity of taxpayers; the preferred measure is income.
The group stresses the ethical aspect of taxation and direct taxation as the best
means (at least in principle) for achieving ethical ends. The group is generally
congenial to progressive taxation, and much of its attention is focused on the
relation of taxation to inequality of income. However, we shall not regard
support of the progressive principle as a criterion for inclusion in the group.

The second group, whom we call the *opportunists,* gives great weight to
the practical considerations of collecting revenue with minimum friction and
encroachment on incentives. The political aspect of this preference is suggested in the famous metaphor "most feathers for least squawking." The preferred means is impersonal taxation of consumption.

A third and much smaller group, whom we may label the *direct-expendi-
ture tax* proponents, agrees with the first group that taxes should be personal
and direct and perhaps progressive. Recent formulation holds that governments should not ignore expenditures from wealth as contrasted with income

(living high off of past accumulation). It also holds that taxes should take account of what one does with his income, this being more important than either the source of the income or the amount the recipient has to dispose. Saving is exalted as a disposition to be fostered and one involving a sacrifice that should be weighted along with that of taxation.

The fourth group, resembling in some respects the third, we may label the *functional* school. It recommends so ordering the system that it will least affect production and doing this by levies that strike "windfall" income, that is, income that requires no incentive and makes no return to the commonwealth. The emphasis is economic rather than ethical, though these objectives are usually seen as harmonious. The principal source of such income, it is said, derives from private ownership of natural resources or gifts of nature. Some proponents would add inheritance to this category. The distinctions made in taxing income and wealth should be qualitative rather than (or perhaps in addition to) quantitative ones.

The reviewer concedes that his classification and particularly his labels are not immune to attack. In some sense and in some degree any proposed order for the tax system is based on rational grounds, that of the first no more than the others and particularly no more than that of the third. Moreover, the labels do have some emotional connotations and may prejudice the reader before he examines the content of doctrines. The term *opportunism* is defined in one edition of Webster's dictionary as the "art, policy or practice of taking advantage . . . of opportunities or circumstances," or alternatively, "of seeking immediate advantage with little regard for principles or ultimate consequences." The anticipated criticism of these labels is not without an element of validity, but with this recognized, it seems to the reviewer that their descriptive merits warrant retaining them.

Nature of the State

Public finance has a root in political science as well as one in economics, and some conception of the state and how it makes its decisions is linked to taxation. We may start with the ancient theories of the origin of the state. Our treatment must be very sketchy, with selection dictated by our purpose to buttress a history of tax philosophy.

The idea that the state should be conceived as a covenent among its citizens goes back at least to the English philosopher of the seventeenth century Thomas Hobbes (1588-1679). (Strictly speaking, it was society rather than government which was formed by the first covenent, but we may ignore these subtleties here.)

Although Hobbes was an ardent loyalist, he was hostile to religion and did not wish to defend kings (against parliaments) with divine sanction. Instead, he began his thinking, reflected in his work *Leviathan*, with consideration of what things must have been in a state of nature. Whether this state ever existed

Introduction

as an historical fact didn't particularly matter—if one preferred, he might conceive it as a rhetorical or explanatory myth. All men are motivated solely by self-interest, which in turn is principally an interest in security and power, the latter serving the former. Men have both instincts and reason, the former dictating aggression, the latter accommodation (enlightened self-interest). The state of nature for Hobbes was one of force and fraud—"the war of one against all." To be sure, there were natural laws dictated by reason, but they frequently ran counter to the human passions. Things became so intolerable eventually that the people got together and picked a leader to keep order. The choice was between despotism and anarchy and the people preferred the former. The covenant thus established not only gave the king a monopoly of violence; it gave him all but unlimited power over individuals.

Far more congenial to the rising democratic sentiments of England were the views of John Locke (1632–1704). His *Two Treatises of Government* was published in 1690 just after the Revolution of 1688. However, it, along with his several other important works, was written in Holland where Locke had been in exile.

Locke was a physician as well as a philosopher, and he was introduced to politics through his professional services for the Earl of Shaftsbury, whom he followed in exile to Holland when the Earl was accused of high treason. He was thoroughly steeped in the traditions of Puritanism, including the ideas of natural law, individual rights, religious toleration, and limitations on the power of the state. Locke's role was to present this package in closely reasoned and persuasive writing. He held several minor governmental posts during his life and he drafted a constitution for Carolina (which, however, was not adopted). His influence in America on the Revolution, the Declaration of Independence, and the Federal Constitution was especially profound. He was a scholar with a fine endowment of common sense, and he rarely let his logic get the better of it. This involved him in some ambiguities and inconsistencies.

Locke's first *Treatise* was a devastating attack on Sir Robert Filmer's *Patriarcha,* published posthumously in 1680, in which the latter had defended the divine right of kings with authority beyond challenge or question, tracing its genealogy back to Adam. Locke argued that the consent of the governed was the basic justification for government.

Like Hobbes, Locke found the origin of government in a social compact, but for him, nature was a happy state governed by the laws of nature. Locke insisted that his own state of nature was an historical fact, but his description was of men as they ought to behave according to the dictates of reason. Nevertheless, there were some who did not obey the higher law, and the compact was instituted to provide the necessary sanctions. Inconveniences were bound to arise where every man was judge of his own cause.

Locke envisioned a hierarchy in the division of power: a community is constituted by a majority of its members who set up a government to serve in a fiduciary capacity. The government consists mainly of legislature and king, who check each other. However, the individual has a reserved sphere of his own by natural rights. The image thus depicted, though by no means entirely original, was destined for a great future.

Jean Jacques Rousseau (1712–78), like Hobbes and Locke, found the origin of government in a social compact emerging out of a state of nature. Rousseau is particularly remembered for his admiration of the natural man; the human species was naturally good, and man's later evil ways were caused by the corrupting influences of social institutions, including property. Nevertheless, he conceded the necessity of a social compact to establish the sovereignty of the general will. The general will was above the individual will, and it also differed from the will of all. One passage in *The Social Contract* indicates that it is what the consensus of individuals (the will of all) would be were everybody fully informed and allowed to form his opinion without pressure and without the influence of communication. When people vote, they express both self-interest and individual views of the common interest; conflicting personal interests cancel each other, leaving a pure expression of the general will.[1] But it also appears that the general intention (or perhaps what should be the general intention) can be expressed by a single individual—the perfect legislator.[2] Rousseau was not opposed to pure democracy, with qualifications, but representative or parliamentary democracy had no appeal for him, and he recognized no rights of the individual against the state.

Much of this may sound innocent enough, even if somewhat mystical. In the hands of Rousseau's later followers such as Hegel it could, however, develop into a philosophy which exalted a leader and excessive nationalism, found virtue in war, and made the state an end in itself, regardless of the individuals who composed it. This approach is sometimes described as the organic view of the state.

Surveying the above sketches, the reviewer notes what many others have noted, namely that there is no evidence in anthropology or anywhere else that society and government actually evolved from compacts. The compacts of Hobbes, Locke, and Rousseau were conceived of as social rather than governmental, at least in the first phase of their development. One could make some kind of case for the proposition that constitutions are compacts, but it is not clear how and why they bind the minority. The only thing that is natural about natural rights is that experience seems to demonstrate that "it works well enough to allow them." And the institutions of government seem to rest on much the same foundation. Nevertheless, the consequences of some of these fictions, notably those of Locke, probably have been highly salutary.

1. Jean Jacques Rousseau, *The Social Contract*, trans. Gerard Hopkins, in Sir Ernest Barker, *Social Contract* (New York: Oxford University Press, 1948), pp. 193–94.
2. Ibid., pp. 204–9.

Introduction

On the other hand the organic view of the state, while illuminating, involves the dangerous doctrine that the state can be an end in itself.

The Role of Government

Most extreme in their opposition to government and most extravagant in their concern for the individual are the anarchists. In general, they have extolled the view that all government is identified with corruption and exploitation—and of course, coercion. Democracy is no exception to the general rule, since it, too, involves the coercion of a minority by a majority. Moreover, government is unnecessary; free association constrained only by mutual respect and the advantage of mutual aid will suffice. If any government at all is to be tolerated it should be highly decentralized and at the local level. Property that is the fruit of the laborer's effort should be respected; beyond this, property rights, which constitute the principal concern and purpose of government, are exploitation. Contracts, including the marriage contract, should be enforced only by mutual goodwill and expediency. The anarchists' ideal is an interesting contrast to that of the socialist. The passion of the anarchist is for liberty; that of the socialist, a full stomach. The great evil for the socialist is greed; that for the anarchist, power.

For anarchists and for many individualists who are not anarchists, the view that the state itself is the people in action, a sort of grand cooperative, has no appeal. The state involves a reduction in the control by individuals of themselves and their destinies, and the fact that they may still control their destinies collectively is not much compensation. One often hears Americans speaking as though the government were completely outside themselves, taxing them, policing them for some objective in which they have no part. It is an image of government which was once more commonly held than now.

The Marxian socialists seem at the opposite extreme from the anarchists, but the two have some common ground, agreeing at least that the existing state is an instrument of exploitation, a tool of the capitalists. The party line seems also to have vaguely harbored the idea that the state is an evil and temporary institution, and it was Lenin who coined the classic phrase "the withering away of the state." The Marxian socialists have never been distinguished by a strong emphasis upon egalitarianism. It is true that certain egalitarian phrases can be found in the Marxian literature, and the *Communist Manifesto* does support progressive taxation. But the literature as a whole indicates a principal interest in government ownership of what we would now call "the production function." Any reduction of inequalities that might stem from this is of secondary importance. The attitude of the Soviet Union toward income and inheritance taxes corroborates this interpretation. True, government ownership of the vast production machinery deprives private individuals of a great deal of power, but it offers no assurance of a dispersion of political power or responsibility. Indeed, the continuity required for sustained productive

Introduction

management makes ambitious socialism and democracy unlikely bed-fellows.

Pragmatists such as the institutionalists dislike and distrust the deterministic (fatalistic) element in Marxism. The pragmatists prefer the view that not much of anything is inevitable and that man's future is what he makes it. Some support for this can be found in history since Marx; his predictions were based on early nineteenth-century experience and were perhaps reasonable enough for their time. They missed the powers of adaptation which were destined to develop within capitalism. Thus, the prediction of ever-increasing concentration was foiled by the rise of the service industries and anti-trust legislation; that of increasing misery of the workers, by trade unionism, Fordism, and the welfare state; that of more and more business crises, by Keynes and stabilization measures.

It is fair to say that in countries with developed capitalism and democratic institutions, the influence of Marxism has declined substantially during the present generation. It is significant that John Maynard Keynes regarded nationalization of the British railroads as far down on the list of the ailments of capitalism that concerned him. Instead of jockeying for position on the same road, private enterprise and government now travel different roads. But even conforming to the rule that it is not the duty of the state to do what private enterprise can do as well, governments are finding plenty of scope for expansion.

The Classicists

In general, it is fair to say that the classical economists, as a group, were ardent liberals in their time and might be so classed even now. Most of them favored universal suffrage (with qualifications), and this was perhaps the ultimate test in an era when men of property viewed this innovation with great alarm. They favored birth control, factory legislation (at least as to safety, sanitation, and hours of labor for children), public and private education, and with some disagreement, humane poor laws and labor unions. (Outside of Malthus, they developed very little that was useful in a theory of the business cycle.) Above all, they had a pragmatic theory of government functions and held no institutions sacrosanct on any a priori theory of natural rights. They were opposed to a central collectivism and over-all planning and stood squarely for a plural society. It was not for the government to do what individuals could and would do for themselves. They were opposed to many mercantilist regulations, such as the apprenticeship limitations, on the ground that they were foolish and established special privileges for producers' groups. Many liberals now would take a similar stand. They favored evolutionary change as against ardent revolution.

The other view of all of this is, however, not without a core of truth. By and large it is also fair to say that the classicists (excepting Mill) held a sordid and unimaginative view of the limitations of human nature and of government, that they made all attempts at reforming the economic conditions of the early industrial revolution appear useless with their theory of population, that they glorified profit and capital and made its accumulation the prerequisite for any improvement in the status of the working population (the wages fund theory), that their doctrine provided the rationale for the resistance of badly needed reforms.

Some Neo-Classicists

Of those who might be termed the neo-classicists the most extreme was Herbert Spencer, father of that strange-interlude movement now known as Social Darwinism.[3] Darwin acknowledged his debt to the economist Thomas Malthus, and Spencer sought to apply Darwinian thought to social systems and history. The result has been variously described as a theory of the survival of the fittest, with the successful capitalists playing the hero's role as the triumphant species did under Darwin, or as an attempt to fortify laissez-faire with biology.

In his *Social Statics* and several other books, including *Man Versus the State,* Spencer presented the view that society is an organism analogous to those in the biological kingdom. It is an organism evolving from incoherent homogeneity to coherent heterogeneity. Like Marx he held that the evolution is toward perfection and is inevitable—if governments will but resist the temptation to interfere with it. The only acceptable function of the state is to see that freedom is not curbed by private means. Ruled out are such traditional functions as public education, poor relief, and even the suppression of medical quacks. The latter serve the useful if unwitting function of getting rid of the unfit. Spencer's evolutionary approach produced an individualism that undoubtedly went far beyond that of the classical economists. And in the United States, where so-called big business was faced with a rising criticism and found the doctrine highly useful in defense, it was hospitably received.

Of more contemporary sources we may select Frank Knight's *Freedom and Reform* for a work that eloquently pleads the case for limiting government to a role that preserves and enlarges the freedom of the individual.[4] In this view, the government is extremely limited in its capacity, and what capacity it has should be conserved for vital functions. Moreover, freedom is indivisible; economic freedom is basic to other freedom; free enterprise is essential for civil rights.

Pausing for a comment of our own, we observe the extreme diffusion of power with which we have saddled government to avoid tyranny. First we

3. See Richard Hofstadter, *Social Darwinism in American Thought, 1860–1915* (Philadelphia: University of Pennsylvania Press, 1944).
4. New York: Harper and Brothers, 1947.

have our federal system with its division of power between the national government and the states. At both levels, the executive must share his power with the legislative branch, the latter composed of two coordinate houses. Within each house, power is further diffused among committees, each of which has a powerful chairman chosen solely on the basis of length of service. Coordinate with all of this is the judiciary, checked mainly by its own judgment and discretion. Underneath it all stands the ultimate sovereign, the public, obviously uninformed on many of the complex issues and obliged to express itself through representatives who often submerge issues in favor of a personality contest. It is with this cumbersome mechanism that we spend a third of the national income with budgets that have many imperfections of their own. The wonder is that it works at all. And it works much better, we are constrained to believe, than Knight would concede.

Nor do Knight's strictures about the indivisibility of freedom appear to be borne out by the record. The same Supreme Court which has relaxed its barriers against legislative control of property and business has augmented its concern for personal human rights. As Knight recognizes, freedom to do as one pleases is in competition with the power to do so—sometimes expressed as negative versus positive freedom. If the social security system somewhat curbs the former, it adds bountifully to the latter. And there are many conflicts of freedom. To use a figure of Tawney's, "Freedom for the pike might mean death for the minnows."[5]

---

5. R. H. Tawney, *Equality* (London: George Allen & Unwin, 1931), p. 238.

PART I

*Proponents of the Direct
Taxation of Income and Wealth*

2

Adam Smith

We shall begin our inquiry with Adam Smith and his *Wealth of Nations,* appearing in 1776. Some background on the development of tax institutions and literature before his time is essential.

We know that most of the forms of taxation are very old and that many of the basic methods of modern levies were conceived in antiquity. Thus, we are told that while the Romans had no gasoline tax, they did have a wheel tax on chariots; they had no automobile licenses, but they did charge tolls for the Appian Way; they had no cigarette tax, but they had many excises, of which the levy on salt was an old favorite. Nor is an onerous tax system a uniquely modern experience. The taxes paid by the ancient Hebrews at the time of the birth of Christ were levied to take 40 percent of the national income, most of which was for tribute to Rome. It was not without reason that the Hebrews dreamed of a Messiah who would free them from this load. The French at the time of their famous Revolution were even more burdened, some historians suggesting that the tax for those who paid amounted to 81 percent of their income.

"For some 600 years," says one historian, "mankind through some of its ablest minds, has sought to solve the problem of raising these funds in the most effective and least painful manner, but none of the methods devised has been able to disguise the fact that the money has to come out of somebody's earnings, directly or indirectly."[1] The search for a burdenless tax goes on: governments still print money, devise clever schemes for leaving the burden with foreigners, or cover up the burden on their own citizens. But generally at least, governments as well as individuals have not been too successful in getting something for nothing.

Beginning with the Civil War in the seventeenth century, the British tax system started a pattern that was to continue for a century and a half. National Revenues were obtained mainly from what we would now call consumption

1. Louis H. Cook, "Background of Modern Taxation," *Taxes* 30 (August, 1952): 627.

taxes, including both customs and excises. In the course of the period nearly everything that entered the Englishman's budget was subject to duty either on home or foreign supply: salt, candles, coal, glass, bricks, sugar, paper, newspapers, tobacco, and of course the drinks of indulgence, not only beer and wine and spirits but also tea, coffee, and chocolate. An Irishman of the time entered on his assessment paper: "Take notice, I have cut the throats of all my horses—I have shot all my dogs—I have burned all my carriages—I have dismissed all my servants except my wife, and therefore, I conceive that I cannot be liable to any assessment whatever."[2]

During much of this period England was at war, and the ministers of finance were almost constantly under pressure to supply more money. A few taxes were reduced or repealed on occasion, but this was rare. Thus it was that the income tax was introduced as a last resort and desperate expedient when England was in mortal combat with France under Napoleon.

The English literature on the subject of taxation began to appear about the middle of the seventeenth century and for the most part took the form of occasional pamphlets written by men of affairs to advocate or oppose measures of reform. The mercantilists, as they have been termed, were greatly concerned about Britain's success in international competition and with furthering exports and a favorable balance of trade. Statesmen were expected to guide the economy with wisdom and skill in this endeavor, and an elaborate system of controls had grown up to regulate and stimulate production. Much debate focused on such questions as whether high or low wages were more advantageous as a strategy for success in the international rivalry.

This was the heyday of the benefit theory of taxation, according to which a person should pay for what he gets. Government benefits were thought to be best measured by consumption. Thomas Hobbes in his *Leviathan* expressed this as follows: "The equality of imposition consisteth rather in the quality of that which is consumed, than of the riches of the persons that consume the same. For what reason is there, that he which laboureth much and sparing the fruits of his labour, consumeth little, shall be more charged, that he who liveth idly, getteth little, and spendeth all he gets; seeing that one hath no more protection from the Commonwealth than the other?"[3]

And Sir William Petty expressed much the same idea: "A man is actually and truely rich according to what he eateth, drinketh, weareth, or in any other way really and actually enjoyeth; others are but potentially or imaginatively rich, who, though they may have power over much, make little use of it."[4]

---

2. Quoted in Randolph E. Paul, *Taxation in the United States* (Boston: Little Brown and Company, 1954), p. 77.

3. Thomas Hobbes, *Leviathan,* 3d. ed. (London: George Rutledge & Sons, 1887), p. 158.

4. Available in the *Economic Writings of Sir William Petty,* ed. Charles Henry Halk (Cambridge: At the University Press, 1899), vol. 1.

Adam Smith

Most writers, including Petty, preferred to stress taxes on luxuries, especially luxury imports. But some went so far as to prefer special taxes on the necessities of life, because they thought these taxes would raise the sobriety, carefulness, and efficiency of labor. A revealing passage from the writings of William Temple will serve as an example: "The only way to make the poor industrious is to lay them under the necessity of laboring all the time they can spare from meals and sleep in order to procure the common necessities of life."[5] This seems like a bald rationalization of the interest of the rich, but the view was often enough repeated to indicate that it was taken seriously. It was to be followed in the history of economic thought by many such rationalizations. Nothing could be done for the poor, first, because doing anything would only encourage dissipation; later, because it would be defeated by an excessive birth rate; then, because it would violate the principle of survival of the fittest; and finally, because it would undermine the incentives of those who helped the poor.

Quite different was the view of Thomas Mun (*England's Treasure by Foreign Trade,* 1664), that taxes which the poor pay in the first (or second) instance must ultimately be shifted to the rich. But the strongest statement concerning the matter of incidence (i.e., the final burden of a tax) came from Francis Fauquier, who in his *Essays on Ways and Means* concluded: "The poor do not, never have, nor ever possibly can pay any tax whatever. A man that has nothing can pay nothing, let Governments try what expedients they please to force him."[6] This might be labeled the you-can't-take-a-shirt-off-a-naked-man theory.

Adam Smith (1732–90), the founder of the so-called classical school of economics, is regarded by many as the greatest of the political economists.[7] His life has been described so often that any sketch of it runs the danger of plagiarism. He was born in Scotland after the death of his father and was reared by a devoted mother as her only child. He had a weak constitution and early developed a great fondness for books and a remarkable memory. Educated at Glasgow University and at Oxford, he became lecturer on rhetoric and literature at the University of Edinburgh in 1748, where he began an intimate and permanent friendship with David Hume. In 1751 he was elected

5. William Temple, *A Vindication of Commerce and the Arts* (1758), as quoted in William Green, *The Theory and Practice of Modern Taxation* (Chicago: Commerce Clearing House, 1933), p. 24.

6. As quoted in E. R. A. Seligman, *The Shifting and Incidence of Taxation,* 4th ed. rev. (New York: Columbia University Press, 1921), p. 28.

7. Like most matters concerning economics and economists, this point of view is not unanimous; thus Schumpeter rates Smith as inferior in many respects to his contemporary Sir James Steuart, who was less favored politically and whose doctrines were less suited to the temper of the era. It would appear that timing is a major factor in the success of books. Joseph A. Schumpeter, *History of Economic Analysis* (New York: Oxford University Press, 1954), p. 176.

professor of moral philosophy at Glasgow. In 1759 he published his *Theory of Moral Sentiments,* largely on ethics and psychology, expounding the view that our moral propensities are founded on sympathy.

The *Theory of Moral Sentiments* is of interest to us principally because it illustrates the close association of economics and ethics. The association may have weakened over the years, but it is still quite impressive, especially in public finance. Although Smith became the great apostle of economic freedom, that freedom was to be exercised within the constraints of some law and a great deal of ethics. General rules of conduct were essential, and they had to be of a character that could be approved by the disinterested. Their power could be much enhanced by religion, but they must also have an independent existence. His later work was anticipated with the observation that illusions are frequently beneficial, and so also may be the covetousness with which men pursue wealth. Men who seek great wealth are seldom satisfied when they attain it, but in the process they unwittingly contribute to the real satisfaction of other people. The germ of his cosmological approach to economics can also be found in the *Moral Sentiments:* he was struck by the order of the economic world and its underlying unity with nature. But the order which he saw was also the creation of man observing the rules of moral conduct.[8]

In 1763 Smith became tutor to a young duke, and this gave him an opportunity to travel abroad, particularly in France, where he met and exchanged views with the several leaders of the Physiocratic school of thought. Returning to England in 1766, he spent ten years preparing his *Wealth of Nations,* and it proved a fabulous success. The England of his time and later was waiting for such a book. In 1788 he took a position as Commissioner of Customs in Scotland, thus joining the bureaucrats whom he generally disparaged. He remained a bachelor throughout his life, and it is said somewhat incredibly that his mother was the only woman who had much influence on his career. He was a friendly and generous person and always popular.

Among the general aspects of the *Wealth of Nations* which need concern us here, we may dwell briefly on his much-mooted stress on the motive of self-interest. Consumers get their bread from the baker, said Smith, not because the latter has any concern about their appetites but because he takes thought for his own. Smith is considered by some critics to have taken his cue here from Bernard de Mandeville's celebrated poem, *The Fable of the Bees.* Appearing at the turn of the eighteenth century, Mandeville's verse presented the theme that the progress of mankind is due to its vices. Both luxury and poverty were "meant to be"; without the latter, for instance, who would do the hard work of society? The poem's endorsement of extravagance was particularly

8. See for instance Lionel Robbins, *The Theory of Economic Policy in English Classical Political Economy* (London: Macmillan and Co., 1952); Warren G. Samuels, "The Classical Theory of Economic Policy: Non-Legal Social Control," *Southern Economic Journal* 31, no. 1 (July 1964): 1-20.

shocking to Puritan England, and Mandeville was suspected of being an agent of the distilleries. Smith had no good words for Mandeville but has been accused of appropriating some ideas from his thought.

Smith's dissertation on human motivation has of course proved highly controversial. Smith wrote before the Industrial Revolution and could hardly foresee the abuses of the factory system when unrestrained competition forced (permitted) the unconscionable exploitation of men and especially of women and children. The evidence indicates that he was a man of great sympathy, and his book rarely fails to champion the underdog against the successful merchants and industrialists. He was aware, too, of the importance of people as an economic resource, as witness his proposal to broaden educational opportunities to counteract the stifling effects of a growing division of labor. Moreover, he never argued or supposed that self-interest was the only motivation. If he had merely said that every man had a moral obligation to take care of himself and his family, and had allowed for a mixture of motives beyond this, he might have saved himself a lot of brickbats.

It is not true that individuals always or perhaps even predominantly (1) know their own self-interest; (2) by following their own self-interest serve the public interest; or (3) by following their own self-interest, follow a pattern ordained from above. It has been said that the only way to induce American farmers to follow their own self-interest is to knock them down and serve them in spite of themselves. Group interests and even national interests often motivate individuals, to say nothing of philanthropic interests for all mankind. If Smith recognized this, he underestimated it, as indeed did other classical philosophers, Jeremy Bentham in particular. Anyway, there can be no question that self-interest is a highly powerful motivation and that much of government has been and is devoted to weighting the scales so that self-interest will correspond with public interest. For instance, we punish robbers in part to ensure that crime doesn't pay. A considerable literature has been devoted to this theme and we shall have occasion to recur to it. Moreover, *enlightened* self-interest in the *long-run* is quite likely to correspond with the public interest.

Smith not only reacted with vehemence against the highly controlled economy of the mercantilistic period, but also favored minimum government. His opinion of the competence and potential competence of the bureaucracy of his period was highly unfavorable. For instance: "No two characters are more inconsistent than those of the sovereign and the trader,"[9] or, "Governments are always without any exception the greatest spendthrifts of society."[10] The reason for this incompetence is not far to seek: governments spend other people's money and lack the self-interest motive. (The relative efficiency of

9. Adam Smith, *An Inquiry into the Nature and Causes of the Wealth of Nations,* bk. 5, chap. 2, pt. 1.
10. Ibid., bk. 2, chap. 3.

governmental and free-enterprise operation has also been the subject of profound debate. No doubt evidence could be cited that government at its best commands unrivaled dedication.)

But Smith was far from an anarchist, and he recognized the indispensibility of government in providing security, justice, and public works. Beyond this he started the penchant of the classical economists for citing exceptions to the general rule of *laissez faire.* Smith's list included such items as the post office, compulsory education with some public support, legal limitation of interest, and bank supervision. It can be plausibly argued that the classicists, though skeptical, adopted a pragmatic view toward the role of government that has persisted with no sharp break throughout British and American history. That they had a considerable bias against government, however, is hardly subject to dispute.

Smith's study the *Wealth of Nations* dwelled heavily on the production function and made rather minor contributions to a theory of value and of distribution. It was Ricardo who concentrated on distribution, and even he took no interest in a study of personal distribution, which might have illuminated tax policy. Thus the classical economists laid themselves open to the charge that they were much more interested in processes than in people.

The fifth book of Smith's treatise was devoted to public finance, and it included a review at considerable length of the fiscal practices of England and other countries. He offered a great deal of advice on these matters, advice which was taken seriously by ministers and parliament.

The Smith Canons

Smith is best known for his celebrated maxims of taxation,[11] submitted apparently as guiding stars for statesmen. The idea of maxims (and some of his particular maxims) did not originate with Smith, but his formulation is the one that has come down to us.

First, said Smith, taxes should be *equal* or *equitable,* falling on individuals "like the expense of management to the joint tenants of a great estate, who are obliged to contribute in proportion to their respective interests in the estate." Further, "the subjects of every state ought to contribute to the support of the government, as nearly as possible in proportion to their respective abilities; that is in proportion to the revenues which they respectively enjoy under the protection of the state."

Taxes should be *certain* and not arbitrary, "clear and plain to contributor and every other person." Otherwise the taxpayer may be subject to extortionate administration.

Taxes should be *convenient* as to the time and manner of their levy.

And finally, taxes should be *economical*—that is, not too expensive

11. Ibid., bk. 5, chap. 2, pt. 2.

to collect and not unduly obstructive and discouraging to the tax-payer.

It is the first of these maxims that entitles Smith to a place in the school of thought that features equity in its tax judgments and looks chiefly to net income as the index of tax capacity. It is true that the canon is ambiguous: it suggests both ability to pay and benefits received as the leading principle, and it could be used in support of a gross as well as a net income tax measure. It is also true that Smith lays great stress on his second canon, observing: "The certainty of what each individual ought to pay is, in taxation, a matter of so great importance that a very considerable degree of inequity, it appears, I believe, from the experience of all nations, is not near so great an evil as a very small degree of uncertainty."[12] Moreover, he rejected the net income tax on the score that it would confront insuperable administrative difficulties.

A reading of Smith's fifth book as a whole leads to the conclusion that he was a firm believer in proportionality in taxation. His early interest and grounding in ethics asserted itself in a keen appreciation of the moral aspects of the subject. Compromises against proportional division for the sake of practical considerations were accepted, but Smith was not happy with them. His preference for a house tax based on actual rental values notwithstanding administrative difficulties was a case in point. His concern for uncertainty seems to have been grounded in his observation of tyrannical administration not uncommon in the British experience of his time and notoriously prevalent in France. Smith found himself in a dilemma: good individualist that he was, he resented the thought of bureaucrats prying into private affairs; sensitive to moral values, he perceived that a rational division of taxes was essential at least as an ideal. The importance of certainty as a canon of taxation may now seem remote. But governments of men rather than of laws where whom the taxpayer knows is more important than the statutes are by no means strangers to the modern world.

Many later books on public finance have attempted to revise or supplement Smith's canons. Among the suggestions for addition are *administrative feasibility, stability* or flexibility of revenues, and of course *adequacy*. The economy item is now frequently interpreted to focus on economic growth. But for a short list and a starting point of discussion Smith's canons still serve very well.

Although the renowned first maxim quoted above seems to endorse proportionality in taxation, there is at least one passage in Smith's book which indicates some flirtation with progression. In discussing taxes on house rent Smith observes that the rich (in his day) spent more of their means on housing than the poor, and adds, "It is not very unreasonable that the rich should contribute to the public expense, not only in proportion to their revenue, but

12. Ibid.

something more than in proportion."[13] This should be taken perhaps as an incidental remark, but some critics have regarded it much more seriously.[14] Smith's work in this respect is like the Bible: one can find in it a justification for many points of view.[15]

Like some of the mercantilists who preceded him, Smith held for an exemption of a minimum from taxation and thus could be said to favor degressive taxation (a term applied to proportional taxation of the excess above some basic exemption). But, as in the case of many of the mercantilists, this was on economic rather than ethical grounds. (Here again Smith failed to put his best foot forward, and one suspects that his compassion for the poor may have had a bearing on his conclusions.) His analysis was based on his fourth maxim rather than his first—that taxes should be levied with due regard to their effects on the economy. Thus, a tax on the wages of the ordinary employee was thought to be both useless and inexpedient because "it can have no other effect than to raise them somewhat higher than the tax."[16] As for commodity taxes, "it must always be remembered, however, that it is the luxurious and not the necessary expense of the inferior ranks of people that ought ever to be taxed." As a consequence, "The middling and superior ranks of people, if they understood their own interest, ought always to oppose all taxes on the necessities of life, as well as all direct taxes on the wages of labor." Such taxes "must necessarily diminish more or less the ability of the poor to bring up numerous families."[17] Here we have an anticipation of Thomas Malthus and the fatalistic iron law of wages holding that the price of labor tends to be just enough to enable the population at large to subsist and perpetuate the race. The tax implications of this doctrine, now somewhat obsolete, seem to have been one of its few beneficent features. Actually in Smith's view of population a good bit of mercantilism survived, and some of his passages indicate a belief that a rapidly growing population is the hallmark of a nation's prosperity. It might be argued that since the poor cannot be taxed anyway (as a matter of incidence), no concern need be felt about taxes that they pay in the first instance. But such was not Smith's position, and he favored the repeal of taxes on salt, leather, soap, and candles.

Specific Taxes

In the interest of convenience and certainty (the second and third of his

13. *Wealth of Nations,* bk. 5, chap. 2, pt. 2, art. 1.
14. F. Shehab, *Progressive Taxation* (London: Oxford University Press, 1953), p. 34.
15. Smith's French disciple J. B. Say, noting this negative and ambiguous endorsement of progression, grasped the nettle firmly by the hand. He considered support for a minimum standard free of tax, and preference for taxing luxuries rather than necessities as acknowledgment of the propriety of the progressive principle. Moreover, he anticipated the equal-sacrifice doctrine of John Stuart Mill. *Traité d' economie politique,* bk. 3, chap. 8 (1803).
16. *Wealth of Nations,* bk. 5, chap. 2, art. 3.
17. All three quotations, ibid., art. 4.

tax objectives) Smith felt obliged to order his tax system largely on considerations of administration. Thus he noted that a capitation tax measured by income would be more equitable than a flat tax per head or even one adjusted to rank. But it was clearly necessary to accept the fact that only under extraordinary circumstances would people disclose their economic affairs voluntarily, and that in most cases these facts are not ascertainable otherwise, not at least without an intolerable inquisition. Real estate cannot be hidden from the assessor's view, but the task of maintaining current appraisal of all of it would probably be prohibitive. He did concede the possibility under certain circumstances of administering a direct tax by self-assessment: "In a small republic, where the people have entire confidence in their magistrates, are convinced of the necessity of the tax for the support of the state, and believe it will be faithfully applied to that purpose, such conscientious and voluntary payment may sometimes be expected."[18] Apparently such conditions did not prevail in England during the eighteenth century. Self-assessment is much like the honor system in college; it can work if the conditions are ideal. Notwithstanding the fact that the British have by now achieved a reputation of being extraordinarily good taxpayers, they still minimize the role of self-assessment in the administration of their income tax.

Having concluded that it was impossible to ascertain the necessary facts about income or wealth for direct taxation, Smith was obliged to settle for the best attainable expedients. Here he noted that what a person spends for his house will have a tolerably constant relationship to what he spends altogether, which in turn will have a relationship to his income or other taxpaying capacity. If we cannot determine what he spends for his housing, we might resort to counting hearths and windows. (The latter was regarded as highly preferable, since it avoided the vexation of tax officials entering all the rooms of one's house). However, it was not necessary to rely on these crude and fallacious indices of house rent. Smith thought it possible and preferable to obtain the facts on actual rentals and to base the house tax on these data. Much of the needed information could be obtained by obligatory recording of leases in a public record.

The property tax of England had long been based on rental value so far as real estate was concerned, and such value was apparently the most readily ascertainable of all the facts about wealth. It is interesting to note that the American general property tax, with its heavy concentration upon residential real estate, can be supported (with reservations) on grounds which Smith proclaimed.

Shelter has usually been a favorable target for taxation, and it still is. Our property tax on shelter has been variously estimated at around 25 percent of the cost of this consumption function. Shelter thus ranks with liquor, tobacco, and motor fuel among the components of consumption that are singled out

18. Ibid., art. 2.

for special punishment by the tax system. That shelter merits its position in this list is to say the least doubtful. Like motor fuel it can be said to enjoy some special benefits from government, but these are usually dismissed as minor. Housing is properly regarded from the social point of view as one of the top amenities of life, and especially important in terms of an environment for children. It makes no sense to teach high values of living in good schools while large families live in a single room at home. The untidy appearance of many of our American cities can be attributed to inadequate outlays on housing. Subsidies for better housing are not uncommon, and more of them are advocated. What kind of paradox is this that we single out for special taxation the very function that we wish to encourage?

The housing tax is generally thought to be regressive because expenditures for shelter are a decreasing function of income (Engel's law to the contrary notwithstanding). And many studies have found that the property tax is impressively regressive—perhaps more so than a general sales tax. However, there is reason to believe that the figures exaggerate regressivity for three reasons: (1) annual data take no account of the fact that some people's income is depressed in particular years below their average; (2) the studies are of owner-occupiers and take no account of the fact that (probably) not all landlord's taxes are shifted to tenants; (3) the figures are in terms of net income rather than disposable income and they take no account of the substantial concessions made to shelter in the federal income tax. The figures also take no account of the imputed value of homes that properly should be added to income.

Whether or not the property tax is regressive, it no doubt bears down with especial severity on old people. Old people as a class are property rich and income poor, and their budgets undoubtedly stress the shelter function more than those of other people. This has been recognized in a few states with a special homestead exemption for the aged.[19]

Although Smith, like most of his contemporaries, despaired of any reform of the British property tax, he was not opposed on principle to taxing the rental value of land. Indeed, he regarded so-called ground rent as uniquely suitable for taxation. Here again, he anticipated a long development in the classical tradition discussed in later chapters.

Smith devoted the greater part of his discourse to taxes on commodities. He distinguished with some rigor necessities from luxuries, noting that the former included not only goods that are necessary for life but also those which the established rules of custom and decency require.

19. Editor's Note: Before his death, Professor Groves played a significant role in Wisconsin's adoption of a statute providing relief for elderly persons when their property taxes became an excessive share of their income. The wide acclaim this "circuit breaker" has received from public finance experts is not nearly so strong a tribute to Groves as is the adoption of similar statutes by a majority of states within a five-year span.

He noted that such taxes are likely to be capricious in terms of income, but the compensating factor for their inequality, he thought, lay in the fact that the power to choose luxuries lay with the consumer.[20] Like many another proponent of these levies he noted their practical virtues: that they were paid with little grumbling and were convenient in time and mode of payment. Of his four maxims, he contended that they offended only the fourth. Here he stressed high administrative expenses, the discouragement of some lines of business, the encouragement of smuggling, and the trouble and vexation caused the taxpayer because of frequent and odious visits by taxgatherers. He conceded that excise taxes are bad for the economy because they "alter, more or less, the natural direction of national industry, and turn it into channels always different from, and generally less advantageous than that which it would have run of its own accord."[21] Here he anticipated a prolonged discussion in the economic literature that is still going on.

He might also have observed that when incidence is taken into account, these taxes have less standing as to "certainty" than at first appears; very few people indeed have any certain knowledge of how much consumption taxes they pay.

Smith regarded excises as necessary, but there is reason to believe that he was not altogether happy with the prospect. Moreover, he spoke out strongly for excluding necessities and confining tariff duties to a few selected articles and strictly for revenue. Here lay some ammunition for the long war that was later to develop over the British tariff on corn. In general, Smith opposed trade restrictions on the plausible and simple grounds that territorial division of labor is as beneficial as any other kind. It never pays a person or a state to produce for himself or itself what others can produce more cheaply.

All Taxes out of Income

Early in his comments on taxation Smith observed that all taxes come out of income as levies either on rent, on wages or profits, or on all sources indiscriminately (poll taxes and consumption taxes).[22] The proposition has been repeated many times, but the reviewer is not at all clear what it means. Perhaps it means that all taxpayers have more income than taxes and that they will adjust either their private saving or spending or both to accommodate the tax. The proposition thus interpreted is certainly not strictly valid; taxpayers do sometimes have to liquidate past savings in order to meet current taxes. However, most taxes do not most of the time involve forced liquidation. More likely the proposition is based on the idea that the nation as a whole will have more current output than taxes and that it can and will accommodate taxes by

20. As we shall see, it was McCulloch who built heavily on this argument and John Stuart Mill who largely demolished it.
21. *Wealth of Nations*, bk. 5, chap. 2, pt. 2, art. 4.
22. Ibid., bk. 5, chap. 2, pt. 2.

adjusting disposition of income. This appears to be valid except that it must not be extended to include the idea that taxes cannot encroach upon potential capital (reduce current saving). The point is of some importance; if it be true that all taxes are paid out of income, it follows that all taxes are in some sense income taxes. They differ not in their ultimate source but in the way they tap it and with what pattern of distribution. Thus, property taxes are income taxes measured by property, and sales taxes are income taxes measured by purchases, and so on. It is sometimes argued in the United States today that the income tax source is not available to the states because it has been preempted by the federal government. But since all taxes amount to fishing in the same stream, the income tax cannot be preempted until the stream is dry, in which case all taxes are preempted. On the other hand, it can also be argued that there are some limits to the income tax irrespective of the fact that it takes only a fraction of the national income and that other taxes come out of the same source.

Conclusion

One is always impressed in reviewing the old masters how many ideas of later and current tax controversy were included in their exposition, yet how little apparently was entirely original with them. Smith is no exception to this rule. Most outstanding, at least for our present purpose, was his stress on the moral aspect of taxation and its quest for a rational rule of distribution. It is not so much the specific recommendation as the germs of ideas upon which the future is likely to build.

Smith's specific tax preferences, as indicated above, were dictated in no small part by the low level of competence that seems to have characterized British administration in his era. In this regard the state of affairs in France, where Smith had visited, was notorious. In that unhappy country no tradition of taxation by consent had developed, and insufferable tax privileges were combined with arbitrary and tyrannical administration, ripe for revolution. In England, Smith was only a few generations removed from the English revolutions in which tyrannical taxation had figured heavily.

Taxation is an art and a technique as well as a science, and it always needs to be judged against the conditions of time and place. The dilemmas and frustrations which confronted Smith have confronted many others in many countries in many eras. Viewed only from the standpoint of equity, there are many countries today where indirect levies (themselves not free from corruption) can achieve a more rational and equitable distribution of taxation than direct levies. It may be, and probably is, true that techniques have been developed and that conditions are now sufficiently favorable in certain countries, of which Britain is a foremost example, for decisions concerning tax matters to be regarded as largely emancipated from the thraldom of administrative limitation. The development of integrity and competence in civil service, backed

Adam Smith

by an attitude of mutuality between government and taxpayer, is a national asset that can hardly be overrated. Vetoing tax measures because of the difficulty of administering them is in most cases less compelling than doing so on the ground of their failure to conform to acceptable principles. Administration is usually amenable to improvement where violation of first principles is not. And administration of a given tax may often be improved most effectively in the process of attempting to administer it. The point is sometimes crucial in recommending taxes for so-called underdeveloped economies in our own time.

The classical economists have often been criticized roundly on the score that they offered their precepts as ultimate and universal truths, without due appreciation of the fact that the conditions of time and place bear heavily at least on the wisdom of their policy recommendations. Whether and in what degree, if any, they were guilty of this fault need not detain us here. Suffice it to conclude that at least as to taxation the rule of historical relativity is valid. There may be some universal truths in taxation, but they are dwarfed by the constraints of a particular environment.

3

John Stuart Mill

Between Adam Smith and John Stuart Mill, the British income tax was introduced as a war measure in 1798. It was temporarily abolished in 1802[1], restored the following year to remain until the end of the Napoleonic Wars (1815), and reintroduced, ostensibly as a temporary measure, in 1842. The celebrated feature collection at the source appeared as early as 1803. This was an important innovation that considerably circumvented dependence on self-assessment. Income tax debate in Britain as elsewhere frequently mixed with tariff controversy.

The British income tax as early as 1803 took on those distinguishing features which it carried throughout the nineteenth century: collection at the source; a flat rate with an abatement at the bottom of the scale; initial exemption only; no classification except for schedular reporting; property tax features (including the imputed value of owner-occupied houses); no taxation of capital gains.[2] The house tax, improved along lines suggested by Adam Smith, continued in use until 1924.[3]

John Stuart Mill (1806–73), an English economist of the classical school, is credited with authorship of the most complete and exact (though not the most original) exposition of its doctrines. His *Principles of Political Economy,* published in 1848, is distinguished for its exceptional style; it is packed full of paragraphs of fine writing that have provided a storehouse of quotable material for subsequent scholars. This book served as a text in most English universities for half a century. Most remarkable of all perhaps was the fact that Mill devoted only some eighteen months to its preparation.

1. All the early records were destroyed, an act hailed by one observer as proving "that honour still remains, and may it ever remain in the breast of an Englishman." Quoted in E. R. A. Seligman, *The Income Tax* (New York: Macmillan 1911), p. 88.

2. Only in the 1960s have the last two of these features succumbed to substantial modification.

3. Stephen Dowell, *History of Taxes and Taxation in England* (London: Longmans, Green, and Co., 1888) 2: 404; G. Findlay Shirras, *The Science of Public Finance* (London: Macmillan and Co., 1924), pp. 324–25.

John Stuart Mill

Mill's father, James Mill, who had a considerable reputation of his own, was a close friend of Ricardo and Jeremy Bentham. The elder Mill rated intellectual enjoyments above all others, and among his many pursuits he undertook personally the education of his son John. The nature and progress of this unique experiment is the main theme of the latter's autobiography.[4] The elder Mill, like many another reformer, had deep faith in education. The combination of strict discipline, singleness of purpose, and a highly precocious pupil produced astounding results. Mill began the study of Greek at age three, had mastered geometry, algebra, and the differential calculus between the ages of eight and twelve, and at thirteen had covered economics and logic. We are told that he had scarcely any intercourse with boys of his own age. Notwithstanding all this, he developed a generous and balanced personality, maintained his passion for knowledge and intellectual achievement, managed an idyllic married life, produced copiously and masterfully in several fields of knowledge, was elected to parliament, and remained always highly respected and revered by the people of his time and subsequent generations. His marriage, twenty years delayed out of consideration for the husband of his beloved, proved a very intellectual affair, but certainly not lacking in mutual devotion. Mrs. Mill's considerable influence is credited in part for her husband's growing interest in and support for reform movements. If there were any negative aspects of the educational experiment, the first would probably be that Mill never quite succeeded in shaking his father's influence to develop a completely independent intellectual life of his own. Nevertheless, in the annals of intellectual and literary achievement, it would be hard to find a more remarkable man or career.

Mill was perhaps as near as any one could be to the complete intellectual: ideas and their expression were his life; he never hesitated to follow the dictates of reason. On the other hand, his devotion to Mrs. Mill and his sympathy for the underdog indicate an emotional nature of some capacity.

Distribution Control versus Production Control

In many respects Mill's work both as to economics in general and taxation in particular was an extension and refinement of the ideas promulgated by Adam Smith and Ricardo. But one of his innovations, said to be regarded by Mill as his most important and original contribution to economic science, deserves a leading and independent observation. This, according to a recent appraisal, freed classical economics from the thraldom of natural law.[5] Said Mill: "The laws and conditions of the Production of Wealth partake of the character of physical truths. There is nothing optional or arbitrary in them . . . It is not so with the Distribution of Wealth. That is a matter of human institutions

4. John Stuart Mill, *Autobiography* (New York: Columbia University Press, 1948).
5. Robert L. Heilbroner, *The Worldly Philosophers* (New York: Simon and Schuster, 1953), pp. 151–53.

solely. The things once there, mankind, individually or collectively, can so do with them as they like."[6]

The bearing of this on matters of tax policy is obvious. If we let individuals earn what they can in a free economic system we can later recapture much of these earnings for the state according to an independent plan of redistribution without losing the benefit of the original output. Though Mill proposed no very radical application of this doctrine, it had radical implications not lost, it appears, on later generations.

Some critics have thought that Mill overstated his distinction; it may be doubted that the two spheres of economics he spoke about are so mutually independent as his statement suggests. It can be argued that incomes are prices of the factors of production and that interference with factor rewards is not essentially different from taxing production as such. It can be argued that aggregate income itself may be a function of the pattern of production. Nevertheless, Mill's proposition of "capitalist production–socialist distribution" in our modern day has been put to remarkable test by high income and death tax schedules at severely progressive rates. The protests in the name of incentives have been loud and prolonged; but the economic system continues to function somehow and not without a creditable performance both as to output and growth.

Mill himself was dissatisfied with the distribution that he observed in Britain at the time he wrote. In an often-quoted passage he observed:

> If therefore, the choice were to be made between communism with all its chances and the present state of society with all its sufferings and injustices; if the institution of private property necessarily carried with it as a consequence that the produce of labor should be apportioned as we now see it, almost in inverse proportion to the labour —the largest portion to those who never work at all; the next largest to those whose work is almost nominal, and so in descending scale, the remuneration dwindling as the work grows harder and more disagreeable, until the most fatiguing and exhausting bodily labor cannot count with certainty on being able to earn even the necessities of life; if this or communism were the alternative, all the difficulties great or small of communism, would be as dust in the balance.[7]

Mill on Competition

Notwithstanding the above, Mill always conceded the necessity of free competition in the world as it is. And he spoke no kind words for a progressive income tax. His principal objection to socialism was that it would largely eliminate competition. But he did favor a variety of reforms

6. John Stuart Mill, *Principles of Political Economy* (London: Longmans, Green, and Co., 1923), bk. 2, chap. 1, sec. 1.

7. Ibid., sec. 8.

that were strictly in accord with the individualist's creed—the inheritance tax, unearned increment tax, cooperation, peasant proprietorship—and others that were not so strictly in accord—trade unions and the factory acts. More fundamental than any of these he favored, with qualification, universal suffrage.

And Mill was not altogether happy with the nature of competition as he observed it:

> I confess that I am not charmed with the ideal of life held out to those who think that the normal state of human beings is that of struggling to get on; that the trampling, crushing, elbowing and treading on each other's heels, which form the existing type of social life, are the most desirable lot.[8]

There is nothing out-dated about the above quotation. Nor is the alleged over-emphasis upon competition as a motivation necessarily incompatible with the recognition of its essential function.

Benefit Theory

Up to Mill's time the benefit theory of taxation, the idea that people should return to the government according to what they receive from it, had been predominant in tax literature. Montesquieu had phrased the idea neatly with the proposition that "taxes are a payment of part of one's property in order to enjoy the remainder in security."[9] It was so even in the treatment of Adam Smith although the latter also gestured in the direction of ability to pay. Mill did an extremely effective job in demolishing this notion. He observed that the benefit theory had usually been associated with the governmental function of protection and that this by no means encompassed all that governments were expected to do. Moreover, even in the protection function, the poor probably benefit more from government than do the rich because the former are far less capable of protecting themselves. "Government must be regarded as so preeminently a concern of all, that to determine who are most interested in it is of no real importance."[10] Finally, taking a positive stand for ability to pay, he added: "As, in the case of voluntary subscription for a purpose in which all are interested, all are thought to have done their part fairly when each has contributed according to his means, that is, has made an equal sacrifice for the common object; in like manner should this be the principle of compulsory contributions: and it is superfluous to look for a more ingenious or recondite ground to rest the principle upon."[11]

8. Ibid., bk. 4, chap. 6, sec. 1.
9. Montesquieu, *L'Esprit des Lois* (1748), bk. 13, chap. 1.
10. Mill, *Principles,* bk. 5, chap. 2, sec. 2.
11. Ibid.

Proponents of Direct Taxation

Reviewer's Note on the Benefit Principle

It should be added, however, that the term "benefit" as used by Mill is not very specifically defined. It can be given either an objective or a subjective meaning, the former being related to some factor in the individual's welfare, objectively observed (such as greater security), the latter to a preference by him for a given course of public action at a specified price (taxes). If we assume that an expenditure (service) is of common interest in the first sense, it may nevertheless be of greater benefit to the rich than to the poor in the sense that the former would be willing to pay more to have it. This is so because the value of money (diminishing utility) is less for the rich. This idea, developed by the Swedish economists, Wicksell and Lindahl,[12] explains at least why the rich might acquiesce in proportional and perhaps even progressive taxation. And it connects taxation with public expenditures in a way which the classical economist neglected. It also largely identifies benefits and ability to pay.

Going further, the new benefit theories envisioned a transfer of the whole problem of public finance from ethics to economics. Taxes are the prices of public services, and by a bargaining process we might be able to order both the tax system and the public services it pays for. Coercion is always an evil, and its employment should be rigorously minimized. The notion that benefits are indivisible partakes of the organic view of the state where the latter becomes an end in itself.

This approach has recently been reviewed with some favor by Richard A. Musgrave.[13] The latter, following Wicksell, concedes the validity of correcting maldistribution of income before market criteria of tax and expenditure distribution should be applied. He also speaks of certain "merit wants," where as in compulsory education the preferences of the majority are deliberately forced on the minority. Some of this is permissible, but Musgrave, like Wicksell, considers it wise to conserve strictly the use of coercion. Beyond this presumably there will still be allocation for public services and it would maximize satisfaction if each individual as in the market place could order what he wanted and was able to pay for. Attempting a more elaborate exposition and some criticism of Musgrave's approach, we may note the following:

1. Musgrave defines social wants as "Those services that must be consumed in equal amounts by all." This brings out the important truth that in the case of goods that provide general benefits, the participation of a particular benefi-

12. Knut Wicksell, "A New Principle of Just Taxation," in Richard A. Musgrave and Alan T. Peacock, *Classics in the Theory of Public Finance* (New York: Macmillan Co., 1958), pp. 72–118; Erik Lindahl, "Just Taxation—a Positive Solution" and "Some Controversial Questions in the Theory of Taxation," **ibid.**, pp. 168–76; 214–32.

13. Richard A. Musgrave, *The Theory of Public Finance* (New York: McGraw-Hill Book Co., 1959), chap. 1–5. Musgrave traces the development of the benefit theory among continental writers: Pataleoni, Mazzola, de Viti de Marco, Sax, Wicksell, and Lindahl.

ciary does not diminish the benefits received by others. The contrary is true of the private market or the public fee-supported service: what A takes in gas or electricity from the public or private supplier is not available for B.

The reviewer notes, however, that Musgrave's concept is not free from ambiguities. What is the meaning of "equal amounts"? Obviously it cannot mean subjective satisfactions, with the contention that men do not differ in their preferences for public goods. As to objective benefits, the literal statement suggests that these follow heads regardless of income. The proposition that a poor man with four dependents gets five times as much from government as a rich bachelor is arguable to say the least.

2. The benefit analysis is sharply separated from any changes that society may wish to make in distribution of income before taxes. The possibility and desirability of this separation seems dubious. We alter distribution with the tax system not mainly for its own sake but to reduce the opportunity cost of public services. For example, we maintain an army for protection, but this end may be defeated if the cost is so distributed that the oncoming generation is rendered unfit for service.

3. The payment for public services must involve compulsion because none are excluded from the objective benefits of the program. It is possible to regard all this as a bargaining process in which several people decide and agree on their mutual wants and contributions. Thus we may have a situation where A will pay $500 for a given bundle of services if B also will pay $500, and they may agree that each would prefer a larger bundle for which A would pay $500 and B $650. Now introduce C into the bargain; C who wants no part in a public program at all. C may be lying about his preferences, particularly if he has to pay only for what he orders. But even if his preferences are honestly revealed, he cannot be excused from paying for the objective benefits he gets from the program whether he wants them or not.

All of this is more or less conceded by Musgrave, who is thus reduced in his search for optimums to an examination of techniques for voting. As he indicates, it may be possible in probing for consensus to improve upon majority voting.

But any voting system must usually leave a disappointed minority, and the revenue system which follows cannot be supported in terms of social welfare without interpersonal comparisons and value judgments.

4. The rehabilitation-of-the-benefit theory that Musgrave finds in this analysis is thus hardly more than a recognition that public services can be ordered for better or worse by the political process. It is not proposed to distribute costs to the individual according to his preferences (subjective benefit) but according to objective benefit as seen by some consensus of the voters. The analysis is supported on the ground that it affords some special explanation of how the volume of public expenditures can be determined. In this respect it is rated as superior to the simple proposition that public expenditures

should be expanded to the point where the utility of goods forgone in the private sphere equals that obtained in the public sphere, the voting process to do the weighting. The difference between the two explanations, if any, seems hardly of major significance.

5. The rehabilitation-of-benefits proponents make much of the fact that with diminishing utility, high-income recipients may favor high levels of public expenditure financed by progressive taxes. There is no empirical evidence to support this, but even if it be true it only explains why such programs incur less opposition than might be expected.

The conclusion is that the attempted rehabilitation-of-the-benefit theory has been largely unsuccessful.

It may also be noted that notwithstanding Mill's position that most benefits from government are indivisible, extensive attempts are still made to divide them.[14] This operation, to say the least, is full of pitfalls, one of which is the indirect benefits that attend most public outlays. Poor relief, for instance, may principally benefit the rich by adding to their security. Or to return to the subjective approach, one may conclude that poor relief mostly benefits the multitude of kindly folk who don't like the spectacle of starving people in an affluent society.

Equity in Taxation

Taking off from Smith's four canons like many another writer on public finance, Mill greatly elaborated and defined Smith's first principle. In doing this he introduced the psychological concept of sacrifices as the key to equity. He said:

> As a government ought to make no distinction of persons or classes in the strength of their claims on it, whatever sacrifice it requires from them should be made to bear as nearly as possible with the same pressure upon all; which, it must be observed is the mode by which least sacrifice is occasioned on the whole . . . Equality of taxation, therefore, as a maxim of politics, means equality of sacrifice. It means apportioning the contribution of each person towards the expenses of government, so that he shall feel neither more nor less inconvenience from his share of the payment than any other person experiences from his. The standard, like other standards of perfection, cannot be completely realized; but the first object in every political discussion should be to know what perfection is.[15]

14. See for instance Alfred H. Conrad, "Redistribution through Government Budgets in the United States," in Alan Peacock, *Income Redistribution and Social Policy* (London: Jonathan Cape, 1954), pp. 178–264; Rufus S. Tucker, "The Distribution of Governmental Burdens and Benefits," *American Economic Review* 43, no. 2 (May 1953): 518–34.

15. Mill, *Principles of Political Economy,* bk. 5, chap. 2, sec. 2.

John Stuart Mill

Unfortunately, this passage, like Smith's first maxim, contains an ambiguity. There is a confusion and identification of least sacrifice and equal sacrifice. The difference between the two concepts will be presented in some detail later. Much speculation has attended the explanation of the error. It is possible that in Mill's day the application of any standard of sacrifice with any precision seemed so remote that refinement in thinking beyond Mill's statement seemed not worth the effort.

Mill probably got the idea of reducing tax equity to psychology from Jeremy Bentham's utilitarianism in which he was steeped from an early age and about which he himself contributed an essay. Anticipating a later development of the concept of diminishing utility of income, it was destined for a great future. Whether the idea has clarified or muddied the waters of thinking on progressive taxation and distribution is a moot question to which we shall have occasion to return. Probably, very few people in the past or present would really want to adjust taxes according to people's aversion to them even if such disinclinations could be ascertained.

Progressive Taxation

After the line of rather radical abstract ideas discussed above, one might expect from Mill a fairly radical tax program. It comes as something of a surprise to learn that Mill favored neither an income tax nor (except in special circumstances) the application of progression.

With regard to progressive rates in general, the doctrine, then attracting considerable attention, seemed to Mill "too disputable altogether, and even if true at all, not true to a sufficient extent, to be made the foundation of any rule of taxation."[16] Appropriate graduation did not appear to him "capable of being decided with that degree of certainty on which a legislator or financier ought to act."[17] As for mitigating inequalities in the distribution of income he preferred a more discriminating and selective policy: "It is not the fortunes which are earned, but those which are unearned, that it is for the public good to place under limitation."[18] And with some exceptions, Mill, notwithstanding his observations about distribution, was ready to accept a presumption that where income originates it is earned. Mill's attitude on many matters changed during his lifetime, but there is no evidence that he ever wavered in the view that graduation of income taxes would be "unjust and impolitic."

Mill had no objection to the application of progressive rates to unearned economic gains, and he saw here a legitimate outlet for the urge to restrain the accumulation of large fortunes and restore equality of opportunity. Following Bentham, he opposed collateral inheritance entirely

16. Ibid., sec. 3.
17. Ibid.
18. Ibid.

and regarded bequests to direct heirs as a highly proper subject for taxation—including progressive application. He also made the curious distinction that the right of free bequest is a fundamental attribute of property, but the receipt of property via inheritance is a privilege subject to restrictive legislation.

Moreover, Mill like Smith, favored the exemption of a minimum, and unlike Smith, he included this in his principle of equity. Instead of not being able to tax the poor, it now became a case of not wanting to do so. Up to a certain level of means, he reasoned, the sacrifice required by a tax was "not only greater than, but entirely incommensurate with" that imposed upon additional income. But "the immunity extended to the income required for necessities, should depend upon its actually being expended for that purpose,"[19] and expenditures by the poor for indulgences might be legitimately taxed (through commodity taxes) by the state.

Whether the logic of a minimum exemption requires endorsement of progression over all levels of income has been the subject of considerable debate in the public finance literature. It is the reviewer's opinion that while one of these measures can be supported without allegiance to the other, they both rest on much the same type of analysis and objective. The objective is to reduce the social cost of taxation to a minimum and to allocate resources to achieve social goals which (under criticism) are endorsed by the consensus of public opinion.

Differentiation in Income Taxation According to Source of Income

Much debated in Mill's time in connection with the new practice of taxing income was the question of differentiation of burden among incomes according to source. The idea of differentiation as we know it today in Anglo-Saxon countries calls for a lesser tax on unfunded (earned) incomes than on funded (property) incomes because the former lasts only as long as the recipient can work whereas the latter lasts indefinitely. Accordingly it is said that two incomes, one unfunded and the other funded, should not be regarded as equal before the tax law until the former is allowed a concession which would enable its recipient to provide for retirement and an estate. This might be done in several ways, the simplest of which is to allow a deduction for insurance premiums paid. The British law has used some allowance of this sort from its early years, but the allowance has always been strictly limited by a ceiling. A major issue in differentiation is the treatment it should afford to businessmen who receive mixed income, partly from capital and partly from managerial services.

Mill was a champion of differentiation. People should be taxed, he argued, not upon what they get but upon what they are able to spend. Ideally, a concession should be limited to what a taxpayer actually saves for

19. Ibid.

contingencies, but even a concession based upon what he ought to save and with limits would be acceptable.[20]

Mill carried the case for differentiation considerably beyond the point above discussed. He not only accepted traders for inclusion within a concession, but also suggested that they be given especially favorable rates because of the risk associated with their businesses. In addition to all this, Mill developed the idea that saving in general should be exempt from tax, because in his view where saving and the interest thereon are both subject to levy, a double burden results. The notions of favoring earned income recipients to allow them to save and of property incomes built out of this and other saving, contained perhaps an element of inconsistency; anyway, it threw a deal of confusion into the British debate on the subject.[21] Mill's view on the protection of saving laid the ground for a new school of thought in public finance, which will be discussed presently. Finally, Mill, going much beyond Adam Smith, stressed the suitability of a land rent for special taxation, and as a sporting concession to vested interests, he proposed to confine this type of levy to future increments in the selling price of land (of this also more later).

Specific Taxes

While conceding that an income tax fairly assessed "would be, in point of justice, the least exceptional of all taxes," Mill, like Smith, was impressed by the infringements of equity which must attend such tax by way of administration.[22] "Rents, salaries, annuities, and all fixed incomes," he conceded, "can be exactly ascertained. But the variable gains of professions, and still more the profits of business, which the person interested cannot always himself exactly ascertain, can still less be estimated with any approach to fairness by a tax-collector . . . The tax, therefore, on whatever principle of equality it may be imposed, is in practice unequal in one of the worse ways, falling heaviest on the most conscientious."[23] This position had some warrant, no doubt, but in view of the financial success of the British experiment and its very substantial public support, Mill's negative response is surprising.

Rejecting the income tax and preferring direct to indirect taxes, Mill was obliged like Smith before him to settle for the house tax, the expenditure for housing being regarded as the best available criterion of the citizen's means. People would avoid the house tax principally by more saving, and this would be beneficial for the growth of the economy. It was in accord with Mill's idea

20. Although the point here discussed by Mill was a lively issue in Britain as early as the middle of the nineteenth century, it was not until 1907 that it was incorporated into British law.

21. F. Shehab, *Progressive Taxation* (London: Oxford University Press, 1953), Chapters VIII–IX.

22. Mill, *Principles,* bk. 5, chap. 3, sec. 5.

23. Ibid.

that only expenditures should be taxed. Like most of the other classical economists, Mill regarded capital and more capital as the *sine qua non* of prosperity, progress, and the demand for labor.

However, Mill also accepted and defended indirect taxes because they make the taxpayer less tax conscious. In view of the considerable national debt that had to be honored, minimizing tax resistance seemed very desirable. He rejected the view that indirect taxes are less onerous because the individual can elect to avoid consumption of the taxed commodities, the election being as onerous, he thought, as the escaped tax. However, he argued that taxes on vanities were especially stratetic and burdenless for "when a thing is bought not for its use but for its costliness, cheapness is no recommendation."[24] Taxmakers have traded on this principle for many years, but unfortunately conspicuous consumption is at present insufficient to provide much tax base. Its most prevalent form in the United States today is luxurious automobiles.

Although Mill resisted all sumptuary legislation as an interference with individual liberty, which occupied the pinnacle in his scale of values, he nevertheless accepted taxes on stimulants as desirable. He reasoned to this conclusion as follows: consumption taxes are inevitable, and since they all interfere with consumer's choice, the state is justified in selecting for discouragement those areas that are deemed least important or most injurious.[25] The readiness of his surrender at this point to state interference with individual liberty is unexpected. A tax is not a fine, but the two are first cousins.

Justice

In a discerning discourse on justice, Mill identified this elusive term in large degree with expediency or utility. That course is just which administers in greatest degree to the public good or welfare. Mill applied this conception directly to taxation, noting that some consider an absolute equality of contribution just, while others hold for taxation in proportion to means, and still others support progression. "From these confusions there is no other mode of extrication than the utilitarian."[26] This is not to ignore impartiality. "We should treat all equally well (when no other higher duty forbids) who have deserved equally well of *us* . . .,"[27] and so should society.

The reviewer has no quarrel with this view of the matter, but he notes that it is likely to mean the abandonment of the long quest for an objective rule that would apply equal treatment to those at unequal levels in the vertical distribution of income. Hume had observed that justice and liberty are terms that must be referred for their authority to utility. Identifying principle with

24. Ibid., chap. 6, sec. 3.
25. John Stuart Mill, "On Liberty," in *Utilitarianism, Liberty and Representative Government,* Everyman's Library (New York: E. P. Dutton and Co., 1926), p. 156.
26. Mill, "Utilitarianism," *Utilitarianism,* p. 55.
27. Ibid., p. 57.

expediency, however, is acceptable only if the latter includes those remote and indirect effects of conduct that are frequently ignored when the term expediency is used.

Method

Mill was convinced that there could be a science concerned with human beings and society and that human action would be predictable if we knew all of its antecedents.[28]

Anticipating many later statements of a similar character, he noted that science differs from art: the former deals with means and the latter with ends.[29] We cannot question men's desires; there is no test of the desirable other than that men desire it.[30] The reviewer notes that desires are the butt of as much criticism as means. Mill himself distinguished between what seemed to him higher and lower desires. Because men desire narcotics hardly makes the latter desirable. If economists are concerned with human wants without any appraisal of these wants it does not follow that others are not interested or that the matter is immune to evidence.

"Sound theory is only the formulation for sound practice and whoever despises theory is self-convicted of being a quack."[31] Deduction has its place in reasoning but it can give no secure answers until tentative truth so derived is submitted to the final test of experience.[32]

These unexceptional statements recall the prolonged dispute among economists concerning method and the acrimonious attacks of Sismondi and the so-called (German) Historical School concerning the classicists' approach to economics. Said the critics: Why have the classicists been so blind to the effects of unlimited competition upon people, the latter constituting the most precious capital? The accumulation of wealth *in abstracto* is not the aim of government; rather, it is the participation of all citizens in the pleasures of life which wealth represents. However, the criticism hardly applies to Mill, who at least on some occasions could be as critical of existing personal distribution as anyone.

"The only part of the conduct of anyone for which he is amenable to society," said Mill, "is that which concerns others. In the part which concerns himself, over his own body and mind, the individual is sovereign."[33] This thesis was supported in an eloquent essay on Liberty, not only for its own sake but because diversity is the mother of progress. Mill was as much concerned

28. John Stuart Mill, *System of Logic,* bk. 6, chap. 3.
29. Ibid., chap. 12.
30. Mill, "Utilitarianism," chap. 4.
31. John Stuart Mill, *On Bentham and Coleridge,* (London: Chatto and Windus, 1950), p. 102.
32. Mill, *System of Logic,* bk. 6, chap. 9.
33. Mill, "On Liberty," p. 73.

about the tyranny of society as about that of government. His essay is the charter of nonconformists, and as timely now as when it was written. However, it may be noted that the growing interdependence of mankind has encroached upon the area of individual sovereignty. For instance, suicide today may be regarded as the squandering of social investment in the individual not very different from smashing an electronic machine.

Conclusion

Mill's contributions to tax philosophy are many, and we shall not attempt to recapitulate them here. Suffice it to say that there is not much in the fundamentals of our subject that he did not illuminate. At least three of the four schools of thought used here to classify the tax philosophers stem back directly to Mill's work. He is also an example of a writer with radical ideas and a generally conservative program. The ideas are influential long after the program is forgotten. Even more than Smith (and unlike Ricardo) Mill was a philosopher-economist.

4

E. R. A. Seligman

In many respects the history and environment of taxation in the United States provide striking differences from those in Great Britain. The United States has a federal system, and until the present generation of Americans the predominate part of the public dollar was raised and spent by the states and municipalities. While this is no longer true, the states and municipalities still play a relatively large role in the overall financial picture. This may account for their experiments with inheritance and income taxes not found in British fiscal history. Moreover, the federal government until relatively recent times and except during wars never had a pressing revenue problem. Tariffs and sumptuary excises provided all the revenue needed and on occasion even embarrassing surpluses.

The United States has a constitution which prescribes its system of government and included therein is a provision that direct taxes shall be apportioned among the states according to population. The federal government first employed the income tax during the Civil War, and at least in its application to salary income, such use was sustained by the U.S. Supreme Court. On a second attempt, during the depression of the eighteen-nineties, however, the federal income tax was declared unconstitutional. This was the renowned case of *Pollock* vs. *Farmers' Loan and Trust Co.,* contested in an atmosphere of intense class and political conflict. Few were more critical of this decision than E. R. A. Seligman, who analyzed especially the historical supports for the Court's view and found them full of rationalizations. The Court had concluded that the founders had an income tax in mind when they largely precluded direct taxation by the federal government. The Sixteenth Amendment (1913) removed in large part this impediment to direct taxation. But it still left precluded direct taxation on receipts which the Court might not accept as income.

During most of its history, the United States has been a predominantly rural country. Farmers are a group that create much difficulty in income tax administration.

Finally, we have a government divided as to structure and responsibility between branches; tax laws in the United States are not so much formulated by the Treasury as by congressional committees. This procedure has impressed some critics as one that provides a happy hunting ground for vested interests.

It would not be in accord with our purpose here to present a history of congressional debate and action concerning the income tax. It may be said, however, that the subject was under more or less constant discussion, both in Congress and academic circles following the Civil War. The two arguments against the tax most often repeated were that it would be unadministrable and that it would penalize success. It was said that an income tax would make this a nation of liars and could not be managed without "a system of inquisition and espionage repugnant to American ideas and abhorrent to free citizens."[1] Moreover, instead of taxing income we ought "to pay premiums to men for achieving financial success."[2]

Edward Robert Anderson Seligman (1861–1939) was an American economist noted especially for his many outstanding books on taxation: *The Shifting and Incidence of Taxation* (1892), *Progressive Taxation in Theory and Practice* (1894), *Essays in Taxation* (1895), and *The Income Tax* (1911). This list includes only the more prominent of his works, and several of these went through several editions (the *Essays* setting something of a record with ten editions). These books are notable not so much for their originality as for their breadth of scholarship. The author wrote with perspective and neither time nor language barred his search: when Seligman tackled a subject he typically began with Aristotle and left nothing out. His ability to review and classify literature has not been excelled. His library, which was purchased by Columbia University, was a remarkable collection of 20,000 volumes, said to be the largest private library on economics in the country. He made extraordinary use of it.

Seligman was the son of the founder of a banking firm, J. W. Seligman. After getting his undergraduate degree from Columbia University, he studied for three years in Germany, Switzerland, and France. He later acquired both an LL.D. and a Ph.D. at Columbia, and with this extraordinary equipment he became a professor there in 1888. He was very active in public affairs and served on numerous committees for New York City, New York State, and the League of Nations. Along with Richard T. Ely, he was the principal promoter of the American Economic Association founded in 1885, and during the early 1930s he served as editor-in-chief of the *Encyclopedia of the Social Studies.* He has been described as a "very cautious" liberal.

Public Finance

"Public finance," said Seligman, "is a part of finance in general, and finance is a part of economics. But in a more important sense it is an inde-

1. Quoted from the *New York Sun* by Randolph Paul, *Taxation in the United States* (Boston: Little Brown and Company, 1954), p. 33.
2. Ibid., p. 98.

pendent or separate discipline."[3] It overlaps political science, accounting, psychology, law, and of course, ethics.

The State

Going beyond most American and British writers, Seligman also attempted to develop as the basis of a fiscal philosophy a conception of the state and the place of government activities in the general satisfaction of human wants.[4] Here he distinguished between wants that can be satisfied by individual activity and those that require group organization. Among group organizations to satisfy common wants is the government, unique in its universality of membership and its use of compulsion. Common wants are immeasurable and indivisible, but special wants may also be served by the government. Benefits received and ability to pay are not rival theories, but each principle has its appropriate sphere of action. The state is not an organism, but it is more than a collection of individuals; people are recreated by the groups with which they associate.

This analysis impresses the reviewer as valid and useful, but it leaves out the vital connection between the quantity of public services demanded and tax distribution. This connection is attempted mainly by the writers of continental Europe.[5]

Income Taxation

Seligman's book on the income tax appeared in 1911 shortly before the sixteenth amendment was adopted. He started his treatment with a historical analysis of criteria of taxpaying capacity. Originally, under primitive conditions it seemed that the physical existence of the taxpayer might suffice; here we had extensive application of poll taxes. Next, especially in agricultural communities where land was the principal basis for rank, property appeared to qualify as a satisfactory measure. However, in our day property has obvious limitations: it takes no account of occupational and professional income, of various yields and gaps in yield of different properties with the same value, of indebtedness, nor of intangibles such as goodwill generated by successful business. At a still higher level of maturity we find expenditures used as a measure of capacity or accepted as a presumptive indication of income, but the crudities of this standard are obvious—what a person spends need not correspond with his capacity to do so. At a fourth stage, gross income or product gains acceptance, but this is too impersonal a measure and ignores the negative items that affect capacity. And finally we have net income; this seems to be the flower of the evolutionary process—it is directly related to persons, and it

3. *Encyclopedia of the Social Sciences,* s.v. "public finance."
4. E. R. A. Seligman, "The Social Theory of Fiscal Science" 41, *Political Science Quarterly:* 191–218, 354–83.
5. See Richard Musgrave, *The Theory of Public Finance* (New York: McGraw-Hill Book Co., 1959), particularly chap. 4.

aims at an algebraic appraisal of the taxpayer's current ability to meet tax bills. But even this as we shall see is far from infallible or free from difficulty.

Seligman recorded many reservations and misgivings concerning the application of the income tax in the United States. Like authors previously considered, his main reservations were on the score of administration. Good taxes poorly administered can be less equitable than poor taxes better administered. Achievements in tax administration in the United States had not been reassuring. Moreover there was a dilemma to face: stoppage at the source would minimize the administrative problem, but it could not easily be combined with a graduated rate structure for which there was considerable demand. Successful lump-sum assessment would require extraordinary morale among both taxpayers and administrators.

And there were other reservations: the income tax posed extraordinary problems of definition, and it would take no account of expenditures out of previously accumulated wealth. All of this was to temper the enthusiasm of those who expected an income tax to take over the tax system entirely and who conceived this levy as the wave of the future.

Although Seligman is properly regarded as a foremost early proponent of the net income tax in the United States, his pioneering book on the subject ends with only two firm conclusions: the state should not venture into the field and the federal constitution should be amended to give the federal government the power (at least) to levy an income tax.

It may be noted at this point that Seligman's predictions concerning the income tax, notwithstanding his unchallenged erudition, were considerably belied by later experience. A majority of the states (and some municipalities) have tried their hand with net income taxation with fair success. Indeed, Wisconsin had the temerity to inaugurate a state tax on income in the very year that Seligman's book on the subject appeared. The secret of the success of the Wisconsin tax was state-level civil service administration.[6] The federal government inaugurated its tax in 1913, and although there was some experimentation with collection at the source, this feature, confined to wages, became firmly established only during World War II. The yield and popularity of the tax are indicative of its success. And the tax has since been loaded with a rate structure which would have seemed fantastic to the early critics. Seligman, like Mill before him, had apparently underestimated the potentialities of voluntary compliance with a popularly approved tax and of administrative improvements in response to a new challenge. This is not to say that enforcement is even now without its serious problems or that the warning of these early skeptics can be forgotten.

6. On the strength of this experience and for other reasons Seligman revised his judgment concerning state taxation of income and by 1915 he was advocating a state income tax for New York. *Essays in Taxation,* 10th ed. rev. (New York: Macmillan Co., 1925), pp. 650–59.

E. R. A. Seligman

Justice and Progressive Taxation

One of Seligman's earliest contributions, published by the American Economic Association in 1894, was a treatise on progressive taxation. The year of publication was that of the Supreme Court's *Pollock* decision, and the subject was timely.

Following the usual pattern of his books, Seligman first passed in review the tax philosophies of writers who preceded him, and then submitted a philosophy of his own. So-called compensatory theories were also examined and rejected. These would base progression on the ground that inequalities are frequently the result of privileges conferred by the state. Seligman argued that privileges, like benefits, are not susceptible to measurement.

Privileges are of two kinds, special and general. The taxation of special privileges finds strong sanction in the slogans: "equality of opportunity" and "every man is entitled to the fruits of his labor and no more." The major difficulty is to define the area of special privilege. In all such approaches rent and inheritance figure prominently; but the socialists have argued that all property income is privileged, and others have contended that the sacrifice and irksomeness of acquiring such income is not commensurate with that involved in working.

The doctrine of general privilege asserts that every man is indebted to his forbears or his contemporaries for the major share of his assets. "The organizer of industry," says Hobhouse, "who thinks that he has 'made' himself and his business has found a whole social system ready to his hand in skilled workers, machinery, a market, peace, and order—a vast apparatus and a pervasive atmosphere, the joint creation of millions of men and scores of generations. Take away the whole social factor and we have not Robinson Crusoe, with his salvage from the wreck and his acquired knowledge, but the naked savage living on roots, berries and vermin."[7] Edward Bellamy carried this approach to the extreme of supporting absolute egalitarianism—an equal distribution of the national income. But the idea was not well received by more orthodox socialists who regarded it as both impractical and unjust.[8] Again the problem is that privilege gets mixed with effort in varying degrees. And the approach may be rebutted with the observation that what is a privilege for everybody can really be no privilege for anyone. Perhaps general privilege does provide some underlying philosophical support for progressive taxation, but it is a weak reed on which to hang so ambitious an idea.

Although one would be happy to derive a tax-distribution formula which would insure fair and equal treatment for all, including those at different levels of income, Seligman felt that the search was not likely to be successful. He

7. L. T. Hobhouse, *The Elements of Social Justice,* quoted by H. W. Peck, in *Taxation and Welfare* (New York: Macmillan Co., 1925), p. 179.

8. See Joseph Dorfman, *The Economic Mind in American Civilization,* vol. 3 (New York: Viking Press, 1949), pp. 149–54.

had to content himself with the conclusion that at least progressive taxation is "neither more illogical nor more unjust than proportional taxation,"[9] which latter he did not bother to defend. He observed: "From the equality-of-sacrifice doctrine of itself we cannot deduce any mathematically exact scale of taxation, whether progressive or anything else."[10]

The Faculty Theory

Seligman's most original contribution perhaps was the development of the so-called faculty theory, in which he proposed to take account of power as well as sacrifice in measuring ability to pay. Power relates to production and capacity to produce, whereas sacrifice relates to pleasure derived from consumption. As the reviewer has phrased it elsewhere, the man with faculty has three hands, so to speak, the two biological ones and his bank account . . . The word faculty had been employed in colonial days, and while its use then was mainly associated with property and the property tax, it was extended to cover occupational and professional skills as indicated by their earnings. In 1888 Francis A. Walker had proposed faculty as a tax base superior to property or income.[11] The advantage over income would lie in the fact that ignorance and shiftlessness could constitute no defense under a faculty tax. His idea is reminiscent of the grading system advocated and occasionally employed in educational institutions under which pupils are not rated according to their ability but according to their effort.

Wherever Seligman may have got his idea of faculty, if from anyone, he incorporated in it the equal sacrifice concept of John Stuart Mill and the notion of productive capacity. (The latter he proposed to measure by income rather than by native talent as suggested by Walker.) On the ground that faculty increases more rapidly than income one could support progressive taxation.

Unfortunately faculty is hardly more measurable than sacrifice, which in any event is one of its elements. How do we know that economic power increases more rapidly than income? One does frequently observe that a little success of any kind makes further success more easily attainable. The first mile of the road up the mountain is the toughest to travel. No less a skeptic than Frank Knight seems to have been greatly impressed with the snowballing

9. E. R. A. Seligman, *Progressive Taxation in Theory and Practice,* Publications of the American Economic Association, Monographs, vol. 9, nos. 1 and 2 (Baltimore: American Economic Assoc., 1894), p. 193.

10. Ibid., p. 143.

11. Francis A. Walker, "The Bases of Taxation," *Political Science Quarterly* 3, no. 1 (March 1888): p. 14. Francis A. Walker was a Civil War general, later a collector of the census, and still later professor at Yale and president of Massachusetts Institute of Technology. He achieved a considerable reputation as an economist and is remembered for his criticism of the wages-fund theory and for the development of a rent theory of profits.

capacity of wealth, referring to "the powerful tendency of inequality to increase cumulatively compounding at an enormous rate."[12] But does this tell us conclusively that of two property incomes, one twice as large as the other, the larger has more than twice as much capacity to pay bills, or reproduce itself or to grow as does the smaller one? At the most, the faculty idea seems to lend a plausible argument for some progression in some cases.

Immeasurability is a common failing of tax standards, and Seligman used it to condemn the benefit theory and other theories that he did not like. But when it came to progression he held that "if we can never reach an ideal, there is no good reason why we should not try to get as close to it as possible."[13] "An uncertain rate, if it be in the direction of justice, may nevertheless be preferable to a rate which, like that of proportion, may be more certain without being so equitable."[14] The analysis here is that of Adam Smith with the choice between equity and certainty reversed.

Looking at the matter in 1894, Seligman found himself in the unhappy predicament of having made a case for progression without anything to which it might be applied. A progressive federal income tax was not beyond consideration, but Seligman thought its successful administration would require stoppage at the source which in turn was not compatible with much if any progression. This left Seligman with the death tax as the logical point to apply progressive tax theory. Thus, his tax program in 1894 looked much like that of the more conservative John Stuart Mill.

Incidence

For Seligman, incidence referred to the ultimate burden of a tax. Shifting was a term used to describe the movement of tax burden from its starting point (impact) to its final resting place (incidence). Strictly speaking, incidence is more a matter of economics than philosophy, though some conception of the locus of burden is essential for any serious thought about taxation. The important problem of justice in taxation may indeed be ethical, but until we know (or think we know) the economic effects of taxes, we are in no position to judge them in ethical terms. J. N. Keynes regarded incidence theory as the only positive, as distinct from normative, part of public finance.[15]

We shall not attempt fully to appraise Seligman's work on incidence, much less to present it in detail. As to appraisal, suffice it to say that the historical presentation is unique in the field, and the synthesis and analysis are regarded as among Seligman's top contributions. His was the first modern attempt to

12. Frank H. Knight, *Freedom and Reform* (New York: Harper and Brothers, 1947), p. 9.

13. Seligman, *Progressive Taxation*, p. 192.

14. Ibid., p. 194.

15. John Neville Keynes, *The Scope and Method of Political Economy,* 3rd ed. rev. (London and New York: Macmillan, 1904).

cover the whole subject in detail. Moreover, a very large part of the product has stood the test of time and is still standard doctrine in current college textbooks. Much, however, has been added, and some of his analyses and conclusions have been cogently criticized.

Seligman's criteria (or factors) that determine incidence include all the major items now commonly listed in general treatises: migration of factors of production and the conditions of mobility that make this possible with time, different considerations in the cases of monopoly and competition, elasticity of demand and supply (the latter including conditions of increasing, decreasing, and constant cost), and difference between special and general taxes (the latter involving no possibilities of migration). Much stress was placed on the marginal producer; having no cushion to absorb a tax, he must respond to such levy by ceasing to produce, thus curtailing supply and raising prices. Shifting thus takes place over the dead bodies of marginal producers.

Seligman follows his general analysis with an elaborate account of its application to specific taxes. Here we shall confine ourselves to one of his conclusions, namely that a corporate net income tax will fall on the stockholders. In competitive business such a tax misses the marginal producer, and in the case of monopoly it does not alter the optimum volume. Nevertheless, he conceded at another time and in another connection that business growth and presumably supply are dependent upon a reasonable return after taxes.[16] The point has continued moot up to the time of writing this review, with the logic mostly on the side of Seligman's original conclusion but some historical evidence and much opinion still in dissent.

Since Seligman wrote, controversy associated with this issue continues. On the deductive side, the issue has never been fully resolved because, while profits are not accounting costs, some reward for capital is clearly necessary to insure a long-run supply of it. Thus in the social sense some reward for capital is a cost not different from wages. On the empirical side studies have shown a fairly constant rate of profits after tax, notwithstanding important variations in burden over time.

In the conclusion of his book on incidence Seligman suggested as a guide to tax policy that taxes be selected for the tax system that are either reliably shiftable or reliably nonshiftable. It is an important point and deserves more attention from the tax-makers. Sales taxes particularly suffer from uncertain incidence. As to neutrality in property taxation, he advised that it is not necessary or advisable to attempt to tax all classes of property. If gaps are dictated by considerations of administrative feasibility, they will be filled by the operation of economic forces. Thus, one need not be too concerned about unneutral treatment in exempting personal property while taxing real estate.

16. E. R. A. Seligman, "Income Taxes and the Price Level," *Academy of Political Science Proceedings, 1926*, 2: 19-20.

E. R. A. Seligman

It is much more important that all members of a given class of property be reached in administration than that all classes be covered in the law.

Conclusion

For his time Seligman was a pioneer proponent of rationality in taxation and a leading (though usually cautious) figure in the vanguard attacking the ancient regime in American tax institutions. His philosophical contributions were not his best and they have proved an open invitation for critics. But his wide-ranging scholarship lifted American public finance literature out of its provincialism and provided a broad and firm foundation for its subsequent growth.

5

Jevons and the Marginalists

There occurred during the 1870s, a major innovation in economic thought which had a decided bearing on taxation. This was the development of a theory of consumption and a liaison between economic thought and psychology. Mill, as we have seen, had taken the position that equality in taxation must mean equality of sacrifice, that a minimum of income required for necessities represents such a degree of importance to the individual that it should be spared all burden, and that importance of income decreases as income increases, though in too uncertain proportions to justify progressive taxation.

This line of analysis undoubtedly received much impetus from the hedonistic bent which was introduced in economics during the 1870s. Chief credit for the introduction is usually given to the English economist William Stanley Jevons and the Austrian economist Karl Menger, whose works appeared almost simultaneously in 1871. It was also independently conceived by the French economist Leon Walras in 1874, and original formulation is now credited to the German Hermann Gossen, whose work in 1854 had attracted little attention when it appeared. Jevons' exposition was psychological and Walras' mathematical. The new doctrine was a revolt against cost-of-production theories of value, and it was argued that it is utility along with scarcity that accounts for the power of goods in exchange. As one acquires more of a good, at least at any given time, the importance of successive increments decreases. Subjective values of increments differ among men in given situations, and this explains exchange. Where exchange is possible, one will attempt to dispose of and acquire goods to the point where the marginal utilities of all varieties is equal and a matter of indifference. Added later was the idea of the disutility of labor, the rising curve of which intersects the falling curve of utility to determine the quantity of work performed. Later development also included the application of marginalism to explain the productivity and rewards of factors of production.

Walras worked out a circulation model to prove that a competitive free market system with qualifications maximizes satisfactions. This is regarded as the starting point in what has come to be called welfare economics.

Jevons and the Marginalists

All of this was positive rather than normative. It makes no pretext that consumers' tastes must go unchallenged; one is permitted to argue that the desired is not always the desirable. And the distribution of wealth it prescribes is only economically right, not necessarily ethically right. However, this distinction has not always been clearly propounded. And many critics have regarded marginalism as an apology for the existing order. At least it leaves one evil to shoot at and that is monopoly, including labor unions, which can be accommodated to marginal productivity theory only with some awkwardness. Minimum wage laws particularly have encountered an impediment in marginal productivity theory. Require wages in excess of productivity of marginal workers and the latter will lose their jobs. And if all employers simply raise their prices in response to what amounts to a universal tax, what then?

William Stanley Jevons

Jevons (1835–82), a highly creative and original English economist, took the view that economics should start with a calculus of pleasure and pain. These are qualitative springs of action but they can be quantitatively compared. Here he refers to Bentham whose greatest-good-to-the-greatest-number principle implied that feelings of this sort could be quantified. Jevons had no doubt that "pleasure, pain, labour, utility, value, wealth, money, capital are all notions admitting of quantity."[1] He would hesitate to say "that men will ever have the means of measuring directly the feelings of the human heart, but just as we measure gravity by its effects in the motion of a pendulum, so we may estimate the equality or inequality of feelings by the decisions of the human mind."[2] Moreover, we should not attempt to compare the amount of feeling in one mind with that in another. "The susceptibility of one mind may, for what we know, be a thousand times greater than that of another."[3] However, "questions which appear, and perhaps are, quite indeterminate as regards individuals, may be capable of exact investigation and solution in regard to great masses and wide averages."[4]

The character of wants satisfied at mounting levels of income undergoes a change. Jevons observed this as follows: "The more refined and intellectual our needs become, the less they are capable of satiety. To the desire for articles of taste, science, or curiosity, when once excited, there is hardly any limit."[5]

1. W. Stanley Jevons, *The Theory of Political Economy*, 4th ed. (London: MacMillan and Co., 1911), pp. 9–10.
2. Ibid., p. 11.
3. Ibid., p. 14. Other statements by Jevons are less unequivocal however and lend support to Stigler's contention that Jevons did make interpersonal comparisons. George Stigler, "The Development of Utility Theory," *Journal of Political Economy* 59 (August and October 1950): 307–27, 373–76.
4. Jevons, *Theory of Political Economy*, p. 16.
5. Ibid., p. 53.

Proponents of Direct Taxation

Karl Menger

Karl Menger (1840-1921) in his analysis of demand also avoided the assignment of cardinal properties to utilities and again avoided the utilitarian practice of comparing utilities among individuals. It was the disciples of Menger, including Böhm-Bawerk, who lost these compunctions and "shamelessly" compared "the 'utilities' of rich and poor."[6]

Menger's treatment of the comparative value of different goods, more and less essential, is particularly noteworthy for our purpose. Thus he observes: "The maintenance of life depends neither on having a comfortable bed nor on having a chessboard, but the use of these goods contributes, and certainly in very different degrees, to the increase in our well-being. Hence, there can be no doubt that, when men have a choice between doing without a comfortable bed or doing without a chessboard, they will forego the latter much more readily than the former."[7] Menger submitted a table to illustrate this idea as follows:[8]

I	II	III	IV	V	VI	VII	VIII	IX	X
10	9	8	7	6	5	4	3	2	1
9	8	7	6	5	4	3	2	1	
8	7	6	5	4	3	2	1		
7	6	5	4	3	2	1			
6	5	4	3	2	1				
5	4	3	2	1					
4	3	2	1						
3	2	1							
2	1								
1									

The Roman numerals represent different goods and the arithmetical ones the satisfaction obtained from consuming successive units of each. Thus, one might be indifferent to the acquisition of a third unit of the first good, say food, and the first unit of a less important good, say tobacco. It is assumed in this analysis that different amounts of different goods are all to be obtained with an expenditure of some other resource, notably money.

Note on Satiety

If every need is limited by nature and grows less as the amount acquired increases until a point of zero is reached, does this apply to all goods collec-

6. George J. Stigler, "The Economics of Karl Menger," *Journal of Political Economy* 45, no. 2 (April 1937): 229-57, 240.

7. Karl Menger, *Principles of Economics,* trans. James Dingwall and Bert F. Hoselitz; intro. by Frank H. Knight (Glencoe, Illinois: Free Press, 1950), p. 123.

8. Ibid., p. 127.

tively? Apparently it does in the sense that each of the goods one turns to in the satiation process starts with a lower rank in terms of importance. However, the satiation theory is static rather than dynamic and may take inadequate account of the social nature or relativity of certain wants. We do know that new wants have been created by innovation and advertising. No doubt the medieval kings and nobles enjoyed available goods abundantly, but the poorest peasant today satisfies many wants that they didn't even know about. We know also that some wants are emulative; they arise from the observation that other people enjoy goods that we might also have. Covetousness here is a matter of status or a contagious feeling that we are missing something. Somewhere in the calculus there must be a place too for the important interest in philanthropy—enjoyments that come vicariously through satisfying the wants of others. Economists may be embarrassed by the report that altruistic wants are quite as common as, and little if any less insistent than, egoistic ones. Some have doubted that satiation in any absolute sense is possible for man; he is a discontented animal and the word "enough" is hardly in his vocabulary. Some philosophers (including Adam Smith) have concluded that there is a large element of illusion in much of this, that the capacity of material goods to satisfy human nature is a very limited one. The illusion, if it is that, is a very general and persistent one.

Assuming that the satiation theory has an element of truth, where does saving fit into the calculus? Some saving of course merely looks to the satisfaction of wants in the future and follows the same scale of rating, perhaps with a discount, that characterizes present goods. But there are also acquisitive wants of a different order marked by appetites for power, prestige, and management. Whether these are amenable to satiation is doubtful. If they do become satiated along with the current and future desires for consumption goods, we might have saving as a pure residual—people saving what has little value because they do not know what else to do with their money.

Cohen-Stuart

It was a considerable step from the original marginal utility analysis to the conclusion that the marginal utility of income decreases as the income of one person gets greater, and it was another considerable step to draw from this an ideal progressive pattern of taxation. Nevertheless, before the close of the nineteenth century a considerable number of authors had accepted without much careful analysis the proposition that the diminishing utility principle leads definitely to progressive taxation. The vulnerability of this conclusion was exposed by Arnold Jacob Cohen-Stuart, a Dutch mathematical economist, in 1889.[9]

9. *Bijdrage tot de theorie der progressieve inkomstenbelasting* (The Hague: Martinus Nijhoff, 1889). Translated by Johan C. Te Velde. A part of this work is available

Proponents of Direct Taxation

Stuart demonstrated that on the plausible assumption that utility falls as rapidly as income advances, equal sacrifice is achieved by proportional taxation. Stuart introduced the idea of *proportional sacrifice,* (proportional to the total utility of the parties) and with the additional point of allowing a basic personal exemption in all income tax returns, he derived a moderately progressive scale without abandoning his initial assumption of a unit-elasticity utility curve.

Stuart's demonstration is highly mathematical, but a simple explanation of his approach may be offered as follows: Assume A and B are two taxpayers with incomes of $2,000 and $4,000 respectively, that marginal utility starting with some arbitrary amount falls as fast as income advances, and that a proportional tax of 1 percent is laid on each income. The data below indicate that the proportional tax results in equality of sacrifice:

Taxpayer	Income (1)	Tax Rate (2)	Tax (3)	Utility of marginal dollar (4)	Utility taken by tax (sacrifice) (3×4)
A	$2000	1%	$20	100	2000
B	$4000	1%	40	50	2000

Now A's income and B's income also yield certain total utilities which can be determined by the application of the proper mathematical formula. Since utility is diminishing, A's total utility will be substantially more than half of B's. Assume for the illustration that the totals are 400,000 and 600,000. The model might then appear as follows:

Taxpayer	Income	Marginal utility	Average utility	Total utility
A	$2000	100	200	400,000
B	4000	50	150	600,000

	Proportional tax		Progressive tax	
	In dollars	In units of utility	In dollars	In units of utility
A	20	2000	15	1500
B	40	2000	45	2250

To take an equal amount of utility from each would be to take a larger proportion from A than from B and would leave A less well off relatively than before. Therefore, the tax schedule indicated for proportional sacrifice must be progressive. This is a leave-them-as-you-found-them theory. If now a certain common figure is subtracted from the totals as the utility equivalent of the minimum to be disregarded, considerable progression is indicated.

---

also in Richard A. Musgrave and Alan Peacock, *Classics in the Theory of Public Finance* (New York: Macmillan Co., 1958), pp. 48–71.

Jevons and the Marginalists

This was a highly ingenious innovation and plausible enough, but of course, it does not dispose of two major difficulties: the shape of the utility curve is assumed and is not supported by any evidence; and the analysis ignores the precaution of Jevons and does compare utilities of different people.

6

Edgeworth and Carver

At the turn of the century, two substantial contributions to tax philosophy, one English and the other American, appeared, each lending support to a minimum-sacrifice version of progressive taxation.

F. Y. Edgeworth (1845–1926) was educated at Trinity College, Dublin, and at Oxford. His academic professional career was divided between King's College, London, and Oxford, at which latter post he remained from 1891 to 1922. He was the first editor of the *Economic Journal* (1891) and continued an active association with the magazine all his life. He is said to have been highly reserved in personality and a recluse in his way of life. He remained un-married—one of the few bachelors in the annals of distinguished economists.

Edgeworth was author of no systematic treatment of economics and most of his work consisted of articles in the learned journals. However, his contri-butions to economics were important, including work on the theory of probabil-ity, oligopoly theory, indifference curves, and the "Pure Theory of Taxation" which covered both incidence and the standards for distributing taxes (1889). His celebrated paradoxes associated with the incidence of taxes on one or both of complementary and rival goods still provide puzzles for the sophisticated student of incidence.

Thomas Nixon Carver (1865–1961), an American economist, received his undergraduate training at the University of California. He was professor of economics at Oberlin College from 1894 to 1900, after which he joined the faculty at Harvard and continued to teach economics there until 1932. His interest in taxes was largely incidental to a broader concern about distribution and *Social Justice* (1915). His best work on taxation, "The Ethical Basis of Distribution" (*Annals of the American Academy,* 1895), was characterized by Edgeworth as "an article replete with utilitarian wisdom."[1]

1. F. Y. Edgeworth, *Papers Relating to Political Economy* (London: Macmillan and Co., 1925), 2: 106.

Edgeworth and Carver

Edgeworth on Minimum Sacrifice

Building on Bentham, Edgeworth propounded the view that the logic of the greatest-happiness philosophy supports the principle that the disutility of taxes should be reduced to a minimum, which means minimum sacrifice or leveling incomes to the point where taxes run out. Minimum sacrifice is now sharply distinguished from equal sacrifice, which calls for an equal disutility cost among taxpayers, and from proportional sacrifice, which calls for contributions that will leave taxpayers with the same relative proportion of total utilities as they had before tax. These latter theories, as we have seen, lead to progressive taxation only on certain arbitrary assumptions as to the degree to which marginal utility drops as income rises. With Edgeworth, gone were these difficulties and uncertainties. All that was now needed was the assumption of "what is universally admitted"[2] namely that income does diminish in importance, at least to some extent, as the amount of it increases. Moreover, minimum sacrifice indicates a definite rate structure, albeit a very severe one. "Minimum sacrifice, the direct emanation of utilitarianism, is the sovereign principle of taxation . . . ."[3]

But uncertainty unfortunately enters by the back door. There are counter-utilitarian considerations which must be admitted to the calculus, among them the effects of extreme taxation on total production, on knowledge and culture, and on evasion of the tax. The rates must not be so high as to deprive the taxpayer of the motive to work and to save. These "reservations reduce the *prima facie* revolutionary dictates of pure utilitarianism to the limits of common sense."[4]

Edgeworth was not greatly troubled by the apparent fact that ultimate decisions as to tax rates must be devoid of numerical precision. Taxation decisions are not a definite matter; neither are many other decisions of policy which we are obliged to make constantly—witness the estimates of damages by a jury in a law case or the grading of contestants in academic competition.

If the minimum sacrifice principle seems radical in its implication, equal sacrifice could be as much so, depending on assumptions as to the utility curve. One need not assume that the curve drops proportionately as income rises; indeed there are strong grounds for the view that it drops faster than the income curve rises and that this tendency is particularly prevalent at the top. All sacrifice theories have to be tempered in application by considerations of practical consequences.

Digression on Utilitarianism

Utilitarianism is a system of British ethical doctrine tracing back at least

2. Ibid., p. 117.
3. Ibid., pp. 106–7.
4. Ibid., p. 106.

to Jeremy Bentham (1748–1832). Bentham was not primarily an economist, but an attorney and student of law. His most important work was entitled *Introduction to the Principles of Morals and Legislation* (1789). In this book he made utility, the greatest happiness of the greatest number, the goal of society. Although perhaps most influential in jurisprudence, Bentham's doctrine also proved a potent factor in shaping later classical and neo-classical economics. As we have seen, Jevons and Edgeworth built directly on Bentham.

"Nature," said Benthan, "has placed mankind under the governance of two sovereign masters, pain and pleasure."[5] Pleasures have several dimensions, among them intensity, duration, certainty, and propinquity. In a rough way all individuals have equal capacity to experience pleasures, and they are sufficiently measurable so that they can be totaled and compared.

Bentham above all was interested in the method of social studies and concluded that it must be empirical. Natural law and intuitional sources of dogma were out the window; we should judge policies and institutions solely by whether they work beneficiently. As to source of authority, the declarations of the American and French revolutions were ridiculed. Not that their conclusions were necessarily incorrect, only that like all principles they had to meet the test of reason and experience. Property, monogamy, minimal government, and even inequality could be defended but on new sanctions. To the view that a person has a natural right to the fruits of his own labor the answer is that he has no right to anything unless it can be established that his possession on balance and in the long run will add more to the well-being of the community than it will detract.

It is the business of the legislator to produce a harmony between private and public interest. This is one of the main reasons for punishing crime, that is, to make it unprofitable. The older ethics had regarded punishment as retaliation—getting even with the criminal. This had been affirmed in unequivocal terms by reformers as enlightened as Mohammed and Confucius. The utilitarian sanctions for punishment in addition to the one previously stated are safety, reform of the prisoner, and deterrence. If these be absent the utilitarian is unmoved by the claim that justice requires "getting even with the criminal."

The ethics of utilitarianism extends the obligations of a human being at least as far as all human kind. This again is a departure from the ancient wisdom. Primitive tribes not infrequently developed a code of conduct much like our own. The unimpeachable observation of treaties was a part of this code. But in general, obligations stopped at the boundaries of the tribe. Robberies, murders, and atrocities outside this limited circle were condoned and sometimes honored. The Old Testament is witness to the fact that this was the view of the ancient Hebrews.

5. Jeremy Bentham, *An Introduction to the Principles of Morals and Legislation* (New York: Hafner Publishing Co. 1948), p. 1.

A universal morality is difficult to apply. Taken literally it seems to mean that one has no more obligation to his own brother or next door neighbor than "to some Hottentot" on the other side of the world. But with the aid of a little rationalization the claims of the nearer good can sometimes be identified with those of the larger good. It works well generally for one to start his improvements with himself, his family, and his neighborhood before he begins on broader circles.

The utilitarians distinguish between the intent and the motive of an act. The intent of an act includes all of its foreseen consequences. The intent may be bad even though the motive is laudatory. The man who steals to save his family from starvation is liable for some punishment even though his motive was beyond reproach. Adam Smith's baker who in pursuit of his own good also serves the consumer should be judged by his intent rather than his motive.

The utilitarian ethics is impersonal and objective. It rejects the relativity thesis that right and wrong are a matter of social mores and vary with time and place. It insists on the universal validity of its moral judgments.

The utilitarian doctrine abounds in logical and other difficulties. To list a few of them:

Bentham's psychology, to say the least, lacked subtlety. It is very doubtful that pleasure and pain or even happiness are the sole motives of conduct. The original utilitarian doctrine did not recognize qualitative differences in pleasures: "Pushpin is as good as poetry."

And whom do we include in the calculus: other nations? unborn? posterity? animals? The greatest-good-to-the-greatest-number principle would seem to sanction multiplication of subjects to do the enjoying. Where does this leave us in search of an optimum population? Mill apparently preferred the highest happiness per head.

The whole utilitarian view assumes the measurability of the immeasurable and a comparison of the incomparable. It is not possible to define an objectively correct distribution of happiness.

Our desires are a product of our social setting and are not above criticism. We are concerned about what men should desire as well as with the satisfaction of the desires they now have. Most men presumably desire to be rich; this is constantly criticized not only on the ground that such desires are said not to lead to happiness, but also because there are said to be higher forms of happiness. A pig can surely be happy in his way.

At one point in his *Critique of Welfare Economics,* I. M. D. Little observes that there is something sound in utilitarianism as long as it remains vague and unprecise, but it becomes nonsensical if one tries to make it exact and scientific.[6] There is considerable wisdom in this remark. Of course it is the "good life"

6. I. M. D. Little, *Critique of Welfare Economics* (London: Oxford University Press, 1949), p. 55.

which is the end of economic as of all other endeavor. All public institutions must be judged in terms of whether or not they serve the public interest. What are the alternatives to the utilitarian approach? One can argue that there is no such thing as the general good or the public interest—only conflicting private interests and individual value judgments. But the most casual observation must suffice to convince that we do and must judge conflicting interests, and we do criticize individual values and try to be objective in the process. Moreover, the great influence of the utilitarians has apparently been on the side of the angels. Its loyalty to rational procedure—testing the evidence—and to pursuit of the public good in terms of individual good, contrasts very favorably in terms of consequences with the intuitional philosophies developed on the continent of Europe.[7]

Utilitarianism, as Little says, gives us a proper approach to public policy questions, but it gives us no certain or verifiable answers. Both its ends and its means are always open to debate. Social scientists supply evidence for the debate and also engage in it directly. Taxation is one area among many where the utilitarian approach can hardly be escaped. In this at least Edgeworth was on the right track.

Carver on the Ethics of Distribution

Carver defended the existing system of distribution as at least as ethically defensible as any other. He conceived the existing system as allocating rewards according to service rendered, with society itself exercising its own opinion of what it wants. If clowns are better paid than teachers, this is because the marginal clown is more serviceable in society's view. Marginal utility and marginal productivity are the benevolent policemen that allocate resources and rewards in a manner that is ethically as well as economically defensible.

The reviewer here must interject more than a pinch of skepticism concerning Carver's optimistic view of free distribution. To say nothing of oligopolistic competition and the weighting of consumers' choice according to purchasing power, free enterprise is power economics with scarcity as the basis of power; at best it is only in the economic, not the ethical sense that each party to the process gets what he deserves. Any rare specimen of a man for instance can collect from the system on his unique gift of scarcity power.[8] The work of J. B. Clark on marginal productivity of factors, by implication at least, endowed distributive rewards with ethical propriety. This is now quite properly criticized as a case of mixing value judgments with scientific inquiry.

It may be the ethical duty of successful individuals, says Carver, to give

7. Gunnar Myrdal, *The Political Element in the Development of Economic Theory*, trans. Paul Streeton (London: Routledge and Kegan Paul, 1953), pp. 53–54.

8. See the excellent discussion of this point by Frank Knight, *Freedom and Reform* (New York: Harper and Brothers 1947), p. 8. The issue is discussed further in chapter 8 of this book.

heavily to charitable and social causes, but the state, in using compulsion, should not go beyond insuring distribution according to service. It is quite in order for educators and religious teachers to preach altruism, but it is dangerous for the state to write such a code of duty into the tax system. Thus it is not correct to say that tax distribution should follow the code which society sanctions for private giving. The state uses compulsion, and when men pay what they do not want to pay this is likely to be repressive. A repressive tax involves indirect sacrifices for everybody.[9]

Carver notes that the evils of taxation are sacrifice and repression; society should keep the sum of these two disutilities as low as possible.[10] Taxation according to equal sacrifice would by definition have no repressive or redistributing effects,[11] but it would not minimize sacrifice as Mill apparently supposed. Upper incomes have an element of rent in them (inherited ability), and they will bear taxes beyond equal sacrifice without repressive effects. This provides justification for a moderate degree of progression in taxation, and what is moderate must always be a matter of sound judgment. Because of diminishing utility, redistribution might yield a gain in human satisfactions, but this must always be balanced against a possible loss through repression in the overall total of utilities.

Blum and Kalven—Critics of Progressive Taxation

We find it strategic to consider one critique of sacrifice theories and of progressive taxation at this stage in the development of our outline. This is a book entitled *The Uneasy Case for Progressive Taxation* and the authors are Walter J. Blum and Harry Kalven, Jr., both professors of law at the University of Chicago. It provides both a comprehensive summary of the literature on progressive taxation and a sharply reasoned analysis of the subject.

The question which the authors pose for their analysis is, "On what grounds is a progressive tax on all incomes to be preferred to a proportional tax on all incomes over a minimum of subsistence?"[12] The framing of this fundamental proposition is itself provocative. Why not put the proposition in reverse? Proportional taxation itself must be defended either in terms of some assumption about utility involving interpersonal comparisons or some other ground which the authors do not bother to submit or support.

The authors first proceed to make some analysis of the fiscal and economic

9. This line of thought is especially developed in Carver's "The Minimum Sacrifice Theory of Taxation," *Political Science Quarterly* 19 (1904): 66–79.

10. T. N. Carver, "The Ethical Basis of Distribution and its Application to Taxation," *Annals of the American Academy of Political and Social Science* 6 (July 1895): 79–99.

11. Edgeworth did not subscribe to this view and his treatment seems more persuasive.

12. Walter J. Blum and Harry Kalven, Jr., *The Uneasy Case of Progressive Taxation* (Chicago: University of Chicago Press, 1953), p. 4.

effects of progressive taxation (leaving considerations of equity and equality aside). They note that the yield of the progressive feature of the American tax is not very impressive (under one fourth of the total), that it adds heavily to administrative complications (as in the problems of timing and splitting), that it is susceptible to political abuse. The authors make a considerable score here; the price paid for progression, especially in terms of administration, is substantial.

As to economic factors, it is noted that the practice of progression could hamper economic growth either through its effect on incentives (deteriorating the odds of risk) or through reduction of ability to save. The progressive practice could be valuable as a built-in flexibility feature (unbalancing budgets during depressions to compensate for unemployment) but reducing rates during bad times is an available substitute.

Turning to the matter of equity, the authors pounce hard on the vulnerable spots in sacrifice theory. They argue that minimum sacrifice (Edgeworth and Pigou) can have little appeal in terms of equity because "at least where two men are both above the subsistence level, it is strange indeed to have them share a common burden by putting all of it on the wealthy man."[13]

As for equal sacrifice (or proportional sacrifice after Cohen-Stuart), it leads with no assurance to progressive taxation or any particular degree thereof. Sacrifice theory is of doubtful legitimacy anyway because it involves interpersonal comparisons, ignores the fact that wants are adjusted upward as more means are acquired, and above all depends for definite rates upon indefinite psychological magnitudes. Moreover, such theory must assume that what is true for one homogeneous commodity must also be true of money income. This leaves saving and power interests out of the account.

Referring to Seligman's celebrated defense of arbitrary progressive rates on the score that approximating justice is better than sure injustice, the authors make the ingenious rejoinder that possible rate scales may differ among each other more than one of them differs from proportional taxation. They conclude: "It is rash to assume that the certain injustice of proportion is likely to be greater than the uncertain injustice of progression."[14] Proportion might deviate only a little bit from the true scale and severe progression might be much further off the beam.

Pausing for a comment of his own, the reviewer notes that the authors here are back on the trail of (certain) justice in the narrow sense of equal treatment for individuals at different economic levels. It is a trail that leads nowhere and never can. Moreover the argument proves too much. Proportional taxation like progressive taxation is unequal treatment of unequals, and it is open to all the theoretical criticisms which the authors shoot at progressive taxation. In one sense there is no equal tax, unless it be the poll tax (including

13. Ibid., pp. 44–54.
14. Ibid., p. 46.

women, children, beggars, and invalids). And this was so shocking to the conscience of (even) medieval England that it touched off a revolution. Progressive taxation must muster such support as it can from some kind of balance sheet of its effects relating to the public interest. As Mill discerned, arguments about distributive justice must ultimately be resolved in terms of expediency (utilitarian consequences).

Blum and Kalven next consider the possibility that progression might be defended in terms of a social interest in equality as such. They find that the case for equality would seem to rest on the same untenable assumption regarding welfare that had been questioned in treating sacrifice. The distribution of power associated with that of wealth is considered and dismissed on the ground that economic power must be exercised responsibly so long as the discipline of competition prevails, and where it doesn't, we should activate antitrust programs. This is not very persuasive, and nothing at all is said about the political aspect of concentrated economic power with its potentialities for controlling communications such as television, radio, and press.

Respect is paid to equality of opportunity, and it is conceded that this interest might justify a graduated inheritance tax and that this might not be adequate to give children an equal start in life. But this objective is hopeless anyway because the cultural inheritance of children (the influence of their homes and families) is bound to be unequal.

Nevertheless, in spite of the above, the authors are more receptive to egalitarian arguments than to those associated with sacrifice doctrine. In an inconspicuous footnote they observe that uncertainty in rate scales is not so objectionable here:

> While perhaps no two men will agree on how much equality they desire, presumably neither man is making an error in applying his preference. If their preferences are not equally sound, that is a matter for the democratic debate to resolve. In the end the distrust of progression on the ground of uncertainty of the equality standard is only a doubt about the wisdom of entrusting the question of economic equality to the democratic process.[15]

The reviewer is not disposed to quarrel with this last statement except to reassert that support for equality like that for progressive taxation need not be a pure value judgment. Equality can be a means to an end as well as an end in itself. And we do not solve our problems by telling people who seek our guidance that they should prefer what they prefer.

A variant of utility doctrine, advanced by S. J. Chapman,[16] is introduced by Blum and Kalven. Chapman argued that the diminishing-utility basis for

15. Ibid., p. 89.
16. S. J. Chapman, "The Utility of Income and Progressive Taxation," *Economic Journal* 23 (1913): 25–35.

progressive taxation can be given a social twist: "Wants satisfied by the early increments to income are usually more important socially than the wants satisfied by the later increments to income, whether the satisfaction of the former causes more utility or not."[17] Blum and Kalven regard this as a distasteful attempt to set up a moral hierarchy in consumption; they resent the assumption that "the average expenditures of the less wealthy are any more worthy than the average expenditures of the wealthy."[18]

The reviewer's vote in this dispute is for Chapman. Social evaluation, it appears, is inevitable whether we like it or not. What else are Blum and Kalven doing when they concede the wisdom of personal exemptions? What else are they doing when they accept without question the validity of proportional taxation as the alternative to progression? If we are not to charge the rich man more relatively for government than the poor, then why charge him more absolutely? Nothing much else that the rich man buys is priced according to its purchaser's means. Furthermore, what other possible basis than social evaluation can there be for setting the limits to public expenditure? And must not the tax pattern be a part of this evaluation indicating the substitution that choice involves? Chapman may not tell the whole story but he makes the right start.

Conclusion

To return to Edgeworth and Carver, we note that the contrast between their approach to taxation and that of Seligman is noteworthy. Seligman places great weight on the possibility of discovering a formula of tax distribution that can be called just in the narrow sense of equal treatment for all. The Edgeworth-Carver approach throws this overboard, identifies justice with expediency and merely inquires what tax institutions work best in terms of their overall outcome. Not much is left of the equality doctrine except, of course, the requirement of equal consideration. To this reviewer this represents an advance. However, as Edgeworth clearly recognized, this treatment gives no certain answers. As we shall see later, the so-called welfare economists have continued the hunt for certainties with regard to public policy in distribution of economic goods, but it also has been unrewarding. It appeared to Edgeworth that he had achieved some certainties in his standard of taxation, but even this is vulnerable to attack. It is not clear and certain that marginal utility diminishes throughout all ranges of income, and it is clear that all people are not alike in their hedonistic reactions.

In the reviewer's opinion Edgeworth's and all other sacrifice theories greatly overstress the subjective aspect of wealth and income distribution. It may indeed be doubted that the voter, whose decisions are final in these matters,

17. Ibid., p. 34.
18. Blum and Kalven, *Uneasy Case,* p. 69.

cares much about the individual's attachment to his wealth. One can be sure that very few people would vote, if they could, to relieve anybody of taxation merely because he is inordinately acquisitive. The voter is far more interested in the objective and social aspects of the matter.

Then too Edgeworth's theory provides no connection between taxation and public (or private) expenditures. He simply states that the latter will be less than enough to achieve full equality under least-sacrifice taxation. But where do we stop public spending and why?

7

A. C. Pigou

Following Edgeworth's contribution by a quarter of a century, A. C. Pigou's writings on public finance came at a time when not only the income tax but its progressive feature had become thoroughly entrenched in British finance. Progression in the form of a so-called supertax had been introduced with Lloyd George's famous budget of 1909. This broke a century of inhibitions and is properly described along with the universal franchise as an event of great audacity. There were not a few who viewed it with alarm: when a stone of this sort was once set rolling, no one knew when or where it would stop. "Once the democratic tiger has tasted the millionaires' blood" the end was in sight. And the inhibitions that attended its introduction were softened by the advent soon after of World War I. Still millionaires survived somehow; their powers of adaptation were underrated.

Arthur Cecil Pigou (1877-1959) was successor to the celebrated Alfred Marshall as professor of political economy at Cambridge (1908-43), where he had also received his academic training. Included among his many works are *Protective and Preferential Import Duties* (1906), *The Economics of Welfare* (1920), *Industrial Fluctuations* (1926), *A Study of Public Finance* (1928), and *The Theory of Unemployment* (1933). Outside his academic pursuits, he served on the Royal Commission on the Income Tax which reported in 1919.

Although he could not be called a socialist, not at least in any but the most pragmatic sense, Pigou's work discloses considerable sympathy for the reformist currents that were popular in the Great Britain of his day. In his *Socialism versus Capitalism* (1937) he recommended use of "the weapon of graduated death duties and graduated income tax, not merely as instruments of revenue, but with the deliberate purpose of diminishing the glaring inequalities of fortune and opportunity which deface our present civilization."[1] This is a strong statement, surpassing anything to be found in Wagner whom Seligman described as "socialistic." The book in which it appears was addressed to

1. A. C. Pigou, *Socialism versus Capitalism* (London: Macmillan and Co., 1937), p. 138.

A. C. Pigou

the general reader and "makes no pretense to constitute a learned work."[2] Pigou also offered some support for the capital levy espoused by the British Labour Party in the early 1920s, but his endorsement was highly qualified.

The tone of most of Pigou's work is moderate and rigorously scholarly, analytical, and judicial. During the 1930s he came into considerable conflict with J. M. Keynes, who attacked especially the Pigovian view that cutting wages provides a solution for unemployment. And Pigou was ever and always solicitous about the adequacy of savings.

Investment in People

Pigou laid great stress on the proposition that there may be investment in people—in their health, intelligence, and character—and that if wisely made this is likely to add more to the national product than investment in tangible capital.[3] It was an idea destined for a considerable future. The most lamentable myopia of the nineteenth century was the failure to recognize the social-cost implications of unconscionable labor practices and human slavery. We are still paying dearly for such failures. The new recognition in our own day is witnessed, for instance, by the rapidly rising interest in the economics of education.

Economics of Welfare[4]

Pigou is most widely known for his *Economics of Welfare,* in which he attempted to appraise the effects of many economic, social, and fiscal policies on aggregate national income and its distribution in the short and long run. This work provided much of the stimulus for the current literature on welfare economics. Among other things he called sharply to attention the possible divergence between private and total costs: some production has adverse collateral effects on the community, as when it injures the health of employees; other production yields community benefits beyond those directly associated with its own output. Thus the mere fact that a profitable industry is attracted to a community does not necessarily mean that it adds to the community's economic welfare. Before drawing such a conclusion a social calculus must be added to the private one. These social considerations may justify special taxes (as in the case of the liquor business) or bounties. This innovation of Pigou's, while not of course an entirely new discovery, has been properly regarded as a major contribution.

Pigou proceeded to analyze welfare in terms of the national income and began by distinguishing between economic welfare and welfare in general. The national dividend includes no account of such basic amenities as freedom, health, and security. It equates the desirable with the desired. To answer such

2. Ibid., Preface.
3. Ibid., p. 138.
4. A. C. Pigou, *The Economics of Welfare* (London: Macmillan and Co., 1920).

questions as, Would a nation be better off if it were not so rich? one must surely look outside economics. And even economic welfare may be but roughly
approximated in any available measure. For one thing, the statisticians have the
same difficulty as the tax laws in drawing the line between production and consumption expense. High output may be deceptive if it involves congregation
in large cities with their heavy operating expense and the loss of time and money getting to work.

Pigou further expounded certain principles of welfare, observing that,
other things being equal and subject to some qualifications, economic welfare
will be greater (1) the larger the stream of aggregate real income, (2) the more
equally it is distributed, (3) the more steadily it flows, and (4) the less aggregate dissatisfactions at the cost of which it is generated.

All of this was persuasive, but as we shall see, it did not reduce to an indis-
putable scientific truth the proposition that, other things aside, equality of
distribution would maximize welfare. Involved in this issue is the matter of interpersonal comparisons.

In general, desires for goods, says Pigou, may be assumed to be proportional to the satisfactions they are expected to yield, but the distribution between present and future tends toward irrationality because people heavily discount the future. The tax system must take this into account; unless it does,
there will be too little saving. Here Pigou's position is strictly in the classical
tradition and contrasts sharply with that of his contemporary and colleague,
John Maynard Keynes.

Following the seminal work of Pigou, a substantial literature has developed
on so-called welfare economics. It has been defined as a branch of economic
science which attempts to apply criteria of propriety to economic science policies. It inquires when and how far we can say with scientific precision and assurance that one situation is economically superior to another. Measurement
of utility is an important part of welfare economics.

It asks such questions as this: Does the change from one policy to another
raise or lower the community's total satisfactions? If we cannot measure particular utilities for a single individual, we surely shouldn't try to do so for a
nation as a whole, since this is but adding individual utilities and involves the
additional difficulty of interpersonal comparisons. We could be sure a re-
arrangement is an improvement only if it makes "at least one person better off
in the sense of moving him to a position he prefers without making others
worse off in the sense of moving them to a position which they do not prefer
to the original. A situation in which A is made better off at B's expense is regarded on this criterion as non-assessable, as it would involve interpersonal comparisons."[5] We cannot be sure that one situation is better than another unless

5. Kenneth E. Boulding, "Welfare Economics," in *A Survey of Contemporary Economics,* (Homewood, Ill.: Richard D. Irwin, Inc., 1952), 2: 12.

A. C. Pigou

all gain in proportion, and distribution is not changed. This of course would probably never happen, and this conclusion leaves us with the unhappy observation that economists as economists or as scientists have nothing at all to say about the wisdom of this public policy or that.

Again this view is by no means unanimous; there are several economists of top rank who have never rejected the idea that, other things remaining the same, more equal distribution makes for greater aggregate welfare. Interpersonal comparisons, they say, can be made to the extent needed for practical decisions. We can assume that for large groups of people brought up in the same country, enjoyment capacities are much alike, at least in terms of the averages for the groups. Moreover, absolute proof should not be required for practical decisions. Nobody can prove that anybody beside himself exists, but, nevertheless, everybody is quite sure of it.

A possible way out of the dilemma, it has been suggested, is simply to think of utility in terms of social significance and rely on the democratic process to provide the ratings. Here the question is not whether goods are more important to A than to B but whether goods for A are rated by V (the voter) as more important than goods for B. This introduces the concept of marginal social significance. Assuming consensus on such matters can be determined, all of this can be done without any interpersonal comparisons; we simply rely on an indifference map of all the preference rankings of all the voters. However, this is hardly a way out; if we introduce the factor of intensities of preference we are again back to interpersonal comparisons.

If the view that utility diminishes for the average person at a faster rate than income is not a verifiable proposition, it can nevertheless be accepted by voters as an article of faith supported by some observation. As Simons would say, at least nobody could prove them wrong. However, it is not necessary to base a case for progressive taxation on such slender ground.

Now all of this impresses the reviewer as an exaggerated case of questioning for certainty where certainty in the nature of the case is not to be had. Public policy questions, abounding in number, are not of the sort that yield an answer like those in the back of an eighth-grade arithmetic book. So what? If economists wish to confine themselves to the objective type of evidence which bears on such questions, this is quite understandable and permissible. Other economists may wish to argue the merits of some public-policy question. This also is permissible, though candor in the author's objectives is highly recommended. No one is in any better position to consider the merits and demerits of progressive taxation than an economist who has gathered and weighed the considerable evidence that bears on the subject and who is prepared to analyze the thinking that should be back of a sophisticated opinion about it. As Myrdal has observed, the great debate on questions of this sort emanating from our universities has a profound and beneficent influence on the public.

Proponents of Direct Taxation

Minimum Sacrifice

Much of Pigou's *Study in Public Finance* was devoted to an analysis of what constitutes equity in the field. Starting with equal treatment of equals, he rejected Sidgwick's idea (also Seligman's) that this brand of equity has value in itself. But it has ample support nevertheless in utilitarian terms. Sacrifice is presumably minimized by equal taxation of equals and the sense of wrong and insecurity that would attend arbitrary taxation (including the indirect effects of these reactions on production) are sufficient to condemn such practice.

The validity of equal treatment of equals would seem to be self-evident, but it does involve interpersonal comparisons unless the unknown of personal temperament is included in the measure that indicates equality.

As to the treatment of unequals, Pigou accepted Edgeworth's doctrine of minimum sacrifice with similar qualifications. Equal sacrifice by analogy to equal treatment for all under the legal system is appealing, but it cannot be the ultimate principle; among other limitations it would not support a minimum free from tax. The validity of least sacrifice like the utilitarian objective in general is "given directly by intuition."[6]

Although with least sacrifice accepted as the standard of distributing taxes, the nature of the utility curve has no bearing on the validity of progressive taxation nor its degree; it does re-enter the calculation when a compromise must be effected with the necessities of capital supply. Pigou is of the opinion that the curve must descend quite rapidly at the top of the income scale because the satisfactions in this case are mainly relative—the important thing is not to be very rich but to be much richer than others. Even equal sacrifice accordingly might call for considerable progression. His thinking here is very similar to Edgeworth's.

Pigou answers two of the objections frequently offered to sacrifice principles. With regard to interpersonal comparisons, he argues that "since it is impossible in practice to take account of variations between different people's capacity for enjoyment, this consideration must be ignored, and the assumption made for want of a better, that temperamentally all taxpayers are alike."[7]

Concerning the proposition that people's enjoyment is affected by their having become accustomed to a certain standard of living, he points out that with a continuing tax system, they never will have acquired the tastes that would have gone with the larger income that would have been received had there been no taxes. Thus in applying sacrifice doctrine, reversibility of the utility curve is no problem.

Pausing for a few brief comments of our own, it may be well to observe again that the minimum sacrifice doctrine does abandon the idea of equal

6. Ibid., p. 60.
7. Ibid., p. 76.

A. C. Pigou

treatment (though certainly not equal consideration) of taxpayers. It can be argued that equal sacrifice means equimarginal sacrifice—the last dollar taken from A will always have the same utility as the last dollar taken from B. But C will pay nothing at all, and as between A and B, the equalization is in terms of dollars rather than people. However, whether or not it would be desirable to apply it, any hope of a definitive measure of equal treatment for unequals is fatuous.

Pigou's analysis of utility in the higher brackets gives less than its due to the psychology of the acquisitive economy. Jevonese economics does not tell us that the appetite for power and success diminishes as one gets more of them or that all this is mainly a relative matter. The error is especially apparent in the frequent assumption that the motive for saving is (always) future consumption. The upper ranges of income are immersed in a power, not a utility, economics. Delegation of very large power can better be considered under a trusteeship theory of wealth. The idea is that it doesn't much matter who owns the wealth as long as it is used in the public interest. However, one can hold that even if this theory be accepted, too much concentration of economic power, largely irresponsible, is dangerous.

Repeating a reservation previously recorded, we note that when the voter makes a decision on taxation he does have the well-being of people in mind in some objective sense, but he probably doesn't (nor should) care too much about their personal hedonistic reactions. It is not that A's first trip to the dentist is more important to A than B's second automobile is to B; it is that A's expenditure is more important to the voter because it is in accord with his conception of social objectives. We subject the acquisitive to the same rule as everybody else not only because we cannot distinguish among people by temperament; it is important to note that we wouldn't want to distinguish on this basis if we could.

Returning to Pigou's treatise we recall his acceptance of the minimum-sacrifice principle with qualifications. Application must be tempered by consideration of the economic effects of a tax. Here he introduced a refinement which caught the imagination of the trade. Economic effects are of two kinds: (1) the so-called announcement effects, which have to do with the way conduct is modified by the imposition of a tax, and (2) income effects, which result from the fact that taxes leave payers with less resources to dispose. The distinction is a useful one; it is most readily perceived in the potential effects of taxes on saving. Taxpayers might save less because their will to do so is weakened, or they might save less because they no longer have the same income out of which they can save. The first concerns incentives (substitutions) and the second the wherewithal upon which the incentives work. Minimal announcement effects could be expected with a poll tax, or a lump-sum tax (not to be repeated) or some levy with a low marginal rate (as distinguished from a progressive income tax). However, as to the announcement effects of taxes upon work effort, Pigou concludes that they are not likely to be very significant where work habits are largely conditioned by the institutional organization of jobs. In the case of saving, it is the second type of tax effect which is most important; minimum-sacrifice taxation might seriously undermine the means for saving by those people who are qualified to save, and here lies the principal check on its application.

Definition of Income

Pigou devotes some space to the conceptual and practical difficulties of defining income but he is not at his best here, and with the exception of two of his observations we may pass this part of his book. The income tax, says Pigou, should seek to reach clear income rather than net income; that is, there should be allowances for living expenses of taxpayer and dependents. Moreover, distinction as to family status should not be confined to a flat allowance; it should carry through all of the brackets of income. A percentage-of-income allowance would thus be more appropriate than the usual practice. This is a matter of proper differentiation, and a millionaire with a dependent should pay substantially, not nominally, less than one with only himself to support.

Reviewer's Note on Personal Exemptions

Authors have distinguished several forms which personal exemptions may take: *initial exemption,* which provides an exclusion of minimum income for those whose income does not exceed this amount; *vanishing exemption,* like the initial exemption except that the exclusion is so managed that it disappears gradually with mounting income; *continuing exemption,* which is a constant amount at all income levels; and *tax credit,* by which a constant amount of value in taxes saved is allowed at all levels. To this Pigou added a fifth variety under which the absolute amount of exemption increases as income advances; a simple application would allow a constant percentage of income as the latter mounts.

The case for the percentage-of-income exemption appears persuasive. Of two millionaires, one a bachelor and the other with a family, a per-capita allowance say of $750 makes a hardly perceptible differentiation and is far removed from what rich families may be expected to spend in support of dependents.

The problem of exemptions is intimately related to the concept of clear income often found in public-finance literature. According to this concept, ability to pay begins only after a deduction of expense money sufficient to maintain the taxpayer and his dependents according to some biological or conventional standard. By the same token relative ability to pay must be reckoned in terms of this least common denominator.

But a theory of progressive taxation is also involved. Viewing the matter in terms of sacrifice as does Pigou, it would seem that a diminishing-utility calculation must take large account of the number of persons who divide the income. (Obviously the exemption problem heavily overlaps the question of "splitting," to which some attention will be paid in a later chapter; the Pigou proposal, as a matter of fact, could be designed as a substitute for splitting with little or no change in the result.) But on an alternative theory of progression, which views its application at least in the top brackets as a matter of controlling power, the justification of percentage exemption and indeed of any but a minimum exemption is weak. Power is viewed as pooled by families, and the numbers involved in each case are not significant.

The tax credit commutes the tax saving feature of a continuing exemption to a common value usually derived from the experience of the taxpayer in the lowest bracket. It is like a vanishing exemption that never quite vanishes. It makes no sense in terms of the clear income concept (like basing taxes upon gross income). But on the power approach to taxation it is at least better than a continuing exemption. A vanishing exemption would be still better in principle, but it is an awkward device designed to mitigate the notch problem (big jumps in tax liability at turning points in the scale) inherent in an initial exemption.

The problem is also related to that of broadening the base of the federal tax system. Critics bemoan the fact that well over half of adjusted gross income (net of production expenses) is lost in personal deductions and exemptions. The personal exemptions account for the major share of the lost potential tax base.[8]

Saving

We have already mentioned Pigou's concern lest the tax system unduly encroach upon saving. Moreover he holds that the income tax by nature discriminates against savings. On the assumption that saving involves a postponement of enjoyment, it carries its own sacrifice and should be taxed only in the future when it is enjoyed. Pigou's considerable treatment of this subject is similar to that of Mill. Moreover, as previously stated, saving, according to Pigou, is underrated by many recipients of income because they over-discount the future. An overall expenditure tax would be ideal, but it would probably be impractical to administer.

This is a large order involving plenty of provocation for comment, but we shall defer that until we consider in a later section the proponents of an overall expenditure tax.

Windfalls

Pigou also follows Mill regarding the nature of land rent and its peculiar availability and suitability for taxation. But he is more conservative than Mill

---

8. For a more complete discussion of the problems considered above see Harold M. Groves, *Federal Tax Treatment of the Family* (Washington, D.C.: The Brookings Institution, 1963).

in his recommendations. Increment taxes are considered favorably, but they should be confined to large increments. The smaller ones are not true windfalls, being due to the realization in time of what has been anticipated and purchased at a discount because of its futurity. (Smith buys suburban land, anticipating high rentals in ten years; he pays for all he ever realizes, but he has an increment at the end of the ten year period because the present income is worth more now than the anticipated income was earlier.) A case also was made for a moderate tax on the site value of land. Moderation was recommended because vested expectations (especially capitalization of future prospects by new purchasers) are entitled to consideration.

Writing shortly after World War I, Pigou pays his respects to a war excess profits tax (classed as windfall taxation). During the abnormal circumstances of war, business frequently makes exceptional profits and insofar as they can be isolated, they should be recaptured by the public.

Death Duties

In a difficult but discerning treatment of death taxes, Pigou tackles the old problem of which is more inimical to saving, an income tax or a death tax yielding equivalent amounts? Actually, the comparison is limited to an income tax on investment income and an equivalent death tax, equal both as to revenues and as to distribution. Since amounts extracted from private sources are the same, the discussion can be limited to announcement effects. This is done by comparing the effects of the two types of levies with their lump-sum equivalents. The reviewer finds it convenient to think of these latter as one large poll tax levied in the future as compared with many small ones levied as the taxpayer proceeds through life. The smaller and more frequent levies will be more conducive to current saving to counteract the tax, but the larger one levied at death will not affect the taxpayer's life-time interests. The latter levy will not discourage the taxpayer's current interest in developing economic power. On balance, the death tax is probably the more detrimental but not by a wide margin. Of course, if income from labor were brought into the income tax picture (the reviewer notes) the margin would be larger; in its case much of the proceeds clearly comes from income destined for consumption.

The problem is confused by the fact that capital must be liquidated (sold to other capitalists) in the case of the death tax. But Pigou disposes neatly of this by representing the taxpayer as one among a group of thirty out of which a member will die and pay a tax each year. The issue is thus clearly narrowed to the effect of each type of levy on the property owner's disposition to save. Use of the rvenue by the government is assumed to be identical in both cases.

The author considers the effects of income taxes and death taxes as alternative measures. Take a tax system in which they are combined and in addition property income is singled out for heavier income tax rates than earned income, and we have what seems to be punitive treatment for saving in a country whose philosophers have almost all been highly solicitous about its adequacy. But there are special favors in the British system for capital gains.

Public Expenditures

Pigou goes further than most Anglo-Saxon scholars in connecting taxation with public expenditures. He at least raises the question of how we may determine the optimum aggregate of such expenditures and notes that a balance must be struck between private sacrifices associated with taxation and private satisfaction from public outlays. Ignoring incentives, the more progressive the tax structure and the more uneven the distribution of income, the higher the level of public outlay that can be justified.

Conclusion

With Pigou the tax doctrine of the main line of famous British economists reached its flower. One can hardly fail to note the striking similarities and the common thread that runs through the several fabrics. Thus, at least from Mill on, the underlying philosophy is utilitarian; there is the same reliance on hedonistic criteria, the same skepticism of rent and inheritance, the same concern about inadequate saving, the same preference for the rational pattern of taxation that direct taxation seeks to achieve. And there is also the same unwillingness to regard the state (continental writers notwithstanding) as more than collective action to serve the individual citizen.

On the other hand, it is also tenable to conceive Pigou's work as a very great advance over (or revolt from) the doctrines of Smith and Mill. Shehab expresses this view as follows:

> Thus, for the first time, and after a whole century of *laissez-faire,* which the economist professed completely to support, the coalescence between academic discussion of tax distribution and popular demands was accomplished, a coalescence which the prominence of *laissez-faire* in English economic thought previously made inconceivable. It is this synthesis which characterizes the present system of taxation in England: while it is democratic and popular it has likewise the full support of expert opinion.[9]

However, recalling the debate on welfare economics and other recent expressions of skepticism, one may reserve some doubts about the unanimity of British (or other) expert opinion on any question of economic policy.

---

9. F. Shehab, *Progressive Taxation* (London: Oxford University Press, 1953), pp. 208–9.

8

Henry Simons

Henry C. Simons (1899–1946) was born at Virden, a little mining town in Illinois, and got his education at the Universities of Michigan, Columbia, and Chicago. His first professional position was at the University of Iowa, where he served as Assistant Professor from 1921 to 1927 and from which he went to the University of Chicago. His unfortunate death in 1946 came at the height of his intellectual powers.

Simons's published works were not numerous but they were distinguished by their originality, their vigor, and their brilliant and audacious style. His convictions were very intense and he left all compromising to the politicians. Probably no other American writer in public finance, with the possible exception of Professor Seligman, has been so much quoted and footnoted by foreign authors.

The first of his books, *Personal Income Taxation,* grew out of a doctoral dissertation and was published in 1938. Published also during his lifetime were a considerable number of essays, best known of which is "A Positive Program for Laissez-Faire" (1934). These essays were posthumously gathered into a book called *Economic Policy for a Free Society* (1948). He also left the manuscript of a book published after his death, *Federal Tax Reform* (1949).

His influence extended beyond his books and at the University of Chicago he is regarded as one of the founders of a school of economists who more or less share his views.

General Philosophy

Simons was a liberal in the older meaning of that term and he remained suspicious of the New Deal, Keynesian economics, and most forms of interference by government in the free functioning of the economy. The planning that appealed to him was the sort that would make more freedom possible. To this end he advocated decentralization of power and he remained faithful to his creed in a world hell-bent for contrary goals. As an anti-monopolist he made the trust-busters look conservative. His positive program included size

74

limitations for corporations, compulsory federal incorporation, restricting financial structure to one of Spartan simplicity, and no holding companies (the last with minor exceptions). Many economic historians had heaped praise upon the corporate institution; Simons dared to think that the world might have been better had this legal entity never been conceived. However, he also held that monopolies would soon fall of their own weight were it not for the protecting hand of government (as in tariffs and patent policies). Moreover, large firms are entrenched by advertising, an institution that also involves colossal waste and that should be controlled, among other means, by taxation. He was also skeptical of the worth of powerful unions and thought their achievements for their members, if any, were principally at the expense of the unorganized.

As in the case of business units, many governments are more creative and much safer from the abuse of power than one single governing body. Simons conceived subsidies, which he identified with "vote-buying", as one of democracy's greatest corruptions and especially prevalent at the federal level. "Our federal government (I venture) is far more corrupt in its best years than municipal government at its worst, if one judges by the proportion of outlays (activities) which serve the common interest as against the proportion spent in vote-buying, that is in serving special interests against the common interest."[1] To improve the quality of the tax system, he favored national as against local taxation, but the federal government was to dispense large sums to the states with minimal interference with their freedom—through bloc grants. Government in general, though having many benevolent potentialities, should be closely circumscribed among other reasons because taxes are costly in terms of repression.

Simons had a deep interest in reducing inequalities, and although he thought that this must be at some price in terms of aggregate output, he conceived the goal as worth the price. The price could be minimized if taxes were so imposed as to let production and distribution take their natural course, interceding only after the free market had performed its function. Equality of opportunity also had a strong appeal; here progress was principally a matter of judicious expenditures on health and education. As for justice in the narrow sense of treating equals equally, Simons's sensitivity to this value is not surpassed by any rival's.

Surely an audacious credo this; if it seems a bit unrealistic in our day one can at least wonder if the country would have encountered any worse problems had it had the courage and assurance to try Simons's prescription.

Selection of Taxes

Of all the writers heretofore and hereafter discussed, Henry Simons (with

1. Henry C. Simons, *Economic Policy for a Free Society* (Chicago: University of Chicago Press, 1948), pp. 13–14.

the possible exception of John Hobson) comes closest to favoring a single tax on income—personal income—as the sole support of government. He does concede a place for local property taxes and motor vehicle taxes, but he is unreceptive to other types of levies.[2] Not only should the net income tax provide the major if not sole support for the federal government; the latter should in turn give generous assistance financed by this source to the states.

The selective sales taxes are disliked because they interfere with the free private allocation of resources. Moreover, they have a sumptuary flavor, and while Simons could outdo the Puritans in some respects he had no stomach for the censorship of private tastes by government. His classic footnote on tobacco taxes is typically Simonesque:

> Many liberal persons defend levies like the tobacco tax on the curious grounds that tobacco is not a necessity—the poor people may or can avoid the burden by not consuming the commodity. The position invites two comments. First, it is hardly accurate to say that no burden is involved in getting along without the commodity. Second, it seems a little absurd to go around arguing that poor people could or ought to do without tobacco, especially if it is taxed, in face of the fact that they simply do not do anything of the kind, that the commodity was selected for taxation because they are not expected to do so, and that the government would not get much revenue if they did. The plain fact, to one not confused by moralistic distinctions between necessities and luxuries, is simply that taxes like the tobacco tax are the most effective means available for draining government revenue out of the very bottom of the income scale. The usual textbook discussions on these points hardly deserve less lampooning than their implied definition of luxuries (and semi-luxuries!) as commodities that poor people ought to do without and won't.[3]

This delightful passage deserves two comments from the reviewer. First, society can hardly allocate enormous resources through government without paying some heed to, or making some evaluation of, private allocation. Man is a social animal and all that he does and chooses has to pass social censorship of public opinion whether applied by government or outside it. Secondly, if income tax exemptions are allowed in order to enable citizens to meet their social obligations privately, society may be justified in withdrawing the exemption, so to speak, if it is not so used. The tobacco tax differs from a tax on bread in that the former does not foreclose the taxpayer from taking care of his family according to approved standards. The availability of the choice makes a difference even if it is rarely exercised.

2. He also pays his respects in a footnote to the possibilities of a progressive tax on net worth; taxes on inheritance, however, should be consolidated with the net income tax.

3. Henry C. Simons, *Personal Income Taxation* (Chicago: University of Chicago Press, 1938), pp. 39–40.

Henry Simons

Simons has no more use for a general consumption tax than for a selective one. The opportunism that bulks so large in the support of such measures had no appeal for him at all. Against the sales tax he emphasized the following points: it makes for irresponsible government because it constitutes too easy a solution of the tax system; a good tax (though perhaps hard to pay) is a good defense against bad public expenditures; moreover, the alleged simplicity of a sales tax is an illusion based on the fact that most people have no part in the technical operation of the levy.

The first of these arguments is especially interesting. One may note that sales taxes now have considerable support from the left among people who do not share Simons's skepticism of government and public services. They hold that the difficulties in meeting tax requirements and the resentment which naturally attends payment separated from benefit in time and form, prejudice the voter against adequate allocation of resources for the public services.

Progressive Taxation

Simons supported progressive taxation on the basis of a direct preference for less inequality:

> Taxation must affect the distribution of income, whether we will it so or not; and it is only sensible to face the question as to what kinds of effects are desirable. To do this is to reduce the discussion frankly to the level of ethics or aesthetics . . .
> The case for drastic progression in taxation must be rested on the case against inequality—or the ethical or aesthetic judgment that the prevailing distribution of wealth reveals a degree (and/or kind) of inequality which is distinctly evil or unlovely.[4]

Simons finds sacrifice theory untenable and objectionable on the ground that psychological states are inscrutable and incommensurate with tangible values. Moreover and more important "the case for equality (for less inequality) is enormously stronger than any utility foundation on which it can be rested."[5] More sensible, he thinks, is the so-called social-political approach of Adolph Wagner who would use progressive taxation frankly to improve the distribution of wealth and who would see no point in the practice if the distribution before taxes were acceptable. Simons defends Wagner against Seligman and accuses the latter (quite justly it seems to the reviewer) both of misrepresenting the German economist and of underrating his contribution.[6]

There is an ethical presumption, thinks Simons, supporting equality. Commutative justice dictates that each shall receive according to his contribution to production, but this does not mean that each gets what he deserves.

4. Ibid., pp. 18–19.
5. Ibid., p. 14.
6. See chapter 4, above.

Proponents of Direct Taxation

Distributive justice supercedes commutative justice within families and also within communities (by virtue of charity). Government outlays for the bottom and progressive taxation at the top should follow the mores of distributive justice.[7] Simons concedes that his conclusion on this matter can have standing only as a value judgment—at least no one can prove him wrong.

A Digression on Value Judgments

Many writers, the reviewer among them, have heaved a great sigh of relief as they moved from the involved utilitarian hedonism of sacrifice theory to the simple value-judgment position of Henry Simons. Yet, in the reviewer's opinion Simons reacts too far; he finds the matter at one extreme of subjectivism and carries it to another. Progression is not merely a matter of individual taste although an element of this is inevitably involved. Progression has many economic and political effects concerning which there is or might be available evidence. Most value judgments as such are rational propositions amenable to debate. No one can prove Simons wrong perhaps, but it is worth at least an argument.

There are several types of propositions in the social studies. First, there are verifiable propositions, which of course may or may not have been verified. Second, there are pure matters of taste, which are not even debatable. Whether Queen Elizabeth was a more beautiful queen than Queen Victoria would be an example. Third, there are matters of judgment that are amenable to evidence and lend themselves to debate. Whether Queen Elizabeth was a greater queen than Queen Victoria is a question that would perhaps fall into this group. Both the standard of greatness and the records of achievement would be at issue here. Many propositions fall somewhere between these distinct classifications.

The question of progressive taxation, like that of the protective tariff and many others, falls into the third category. Such questions cannot and need not be lightly dismissed by economists as matters of pure value judgment. They need to be argued at the philosophical level, and the objective evidence that bears on them requires development and analysis. This evidence, moreover, very likely will not all of it be economic; some of it may be political or sociological. This may require some broadening of competence and interest.

In recent years too many economists have dismissed all matters of distribution with the easy observation that this is a matter of social philosophy, social preference, and value judgment. What do economists tell their clients when they are asked for advice as to how to order these preferences? They can tell them to consult their favorite priests and poets. In our opinion this is not a satisfactory answer.

Economic Effects of Progression

Not that Simons ignored the economic effects of progressive taxation; on

7. Simons, *Economic Policy for a Free Society,* pp. 4–7.

the contrary, like other writers, he was much concerned about its effect on the supply of capital and recognized this as the major limiting factor. In a lengthy footnote he attacks the view that oversaving could be a chronic problem or that progressive taxation might take the place of monetary measures to preserve stability and full employment. "Both progress and justice are costly devices—costly, above all, in terms of each other."[8] In 1939 at least, he was clearly casting his vote for a good deal of justice at considerable expense to progress. The importance of growth, he held, could be overrated. And there was more than one way to foster accumulation—for instance, the government might invest some of its receipts in business, functioning quite as well as the investment departments of the better banks and insurance industries that could never become effectively competitive. (The first of these radical suggestions somewhat frightened even Simons, and before publication (1938) he added a footnote in which he hedged it with some precautionary qualifications.) By 1945 he was converted to the view that the primary problem of the economy is production and that the average man has far more to gain from augmented national income than from redistribution.[9] He also stressed, however, that the danger of tax infringement on incentives was much exaggerated. And there is no evidence that he ever wavered in support of substantial progression in the tax system.

To Simons's provocative discussion of capital accumulation in relation to progress one might add that the development of human resources could be as important for growth as abundant capital. Moreover Simons might have returned to his case against uncontrolled advertising, holding it up as a greater enemy of saving than taxes.

Definition of Income

Among the writers so far discussed it remained for Simons to appreciate fully the importance of the definition of income and the inclusions and exclusions of the income tax base. Not finding much adequate treatment of the matter in English he made and recorded a thorough survey of the fertile German literature on the subject.

Among the contenders there was one view that income must represent a recurrent flow of regular receipts and another holding that income is the value of goods and services produced during a period with due allowance for depreciation and depletion of capital. The latter is the concept used by statisticians in estimating national or social income. Neither of these concepts appealed to Simons: the first was rejected because recurrence is always a matter of degree and the second (as well as the first) because it ignores important elements of taxpaying capacity. A third view associated with Irving Fisher and others held that income should be equated with consumption (savings should not be taxed).

8. Simons, *Personal Income Taxation*, p. 24.
9. Simons, *Economic Policy for a Free Society*, pp. 5–6.

This also was rejected on grounds, among others, that savings are frequently an end in themselves (rather than merely postponed consumption) and because exemption of saving could have dire consequences for the distribution of wealth and power. Simons concluded for a definition that would reflect fully the tax-paying capacity of individuals (it need not add up to a meaningful aggregate) and that would indicate in full the changes in economic power between two points of time. This could be stated as follows: Income is "the algebraic sum of (1) the market value of rights exercised in consumption and (2) the change in the value of the store of property rights between the beginning and end of the period in question."[10] The significance of this definition in terms of the much-mooted issue of capital-gains taxation is obvious.

A Note on American Views Concerning Definition of Income

Robert M. Haig was one of the first American writers to formulate and support the doctrine of what he termed the accretion school. His simple and often-quoted definition was, "Income is the money value of the net accretion of one's economic power between two points of time."[11]

Carl C. Plehn dealt with the topic in his presidential address to the American Economic Association in 1923.[12] Income, according to Plehn, is essentially wealth available for recurrent consumption, recurrently received. Capital is wealth standing in space; income is a flow. The characteristics are receipts, spendability without impairing the source of future receipts, and recurrence. The latter does not require regularity but only periodicity. The concept excludes most capital gains and inheritance and gifts. It is similar to the traditional British concept. Damage to an automobile would be ruled out as a nonrecurring expense.

Irving Fisher's ideas were presented in his *Nature of Capital and Income* (1906) and were defended at intervals throughout his lifetime, culminating in a book on the subject in 1942.[13] His idea that real income consists of consumers' satisfactions will be considered in detail later.

Professor William W. Hewett wrote his doctor's dissertation on the subject of income. Hewett accepted the accretion approach for the most part and his principal contribution was in relating individual to social income. Capital gains that are due to changes in market conditions may be counted in social income if we also count capital losses. The two will offset each other; both are in the

10. Simons, *Personal Income Taxation,* p. 50.

11. Robert M. Haig, "The Concept of Income," in *The Federal Income Tax,* ed. Haig (New York: Columbia University Press, 1921), p. 7.

12. Carl C. Plehn, "The Concept of Income as Recurrent Consumable Receipts," *American Economic Review* 14 (March 1924): 1-12.

13. Irving Fisher and Herbert W. Fisher, *Constructive Income Taxation, A Proposal for Reform* (New York: Harper and Brothers, 1942).

nature of transfers; and thus the social income can be defined to equal the total of all individual incomes.[14]

Hewett engaged in some argument with Fisher, acknowledging the latter's concept as a legitimate approach and suggesting that the choice between the accretion and consumption concepts was a matter of convenience and expediency. Since Fisher would exclude depreciation and depletion from his concept, the two approaches could give the same result with differences in timing only.[15]

Simons built on Haig's definition and gave it a much more explicit formulation. He made it clear that definitions of personal income and social income require fundamentally different approaches and that there is no reason to expect an identity between the two. Moreover, he was extremely skeptical of the whole idea of social income, which he regarded as a welfare concept—progress toward the good life and no more measurable. Personal income, however, can be approximated; it involves simply consumption plus changes in the ownership of valuable rights. The regularity or legitimacy of receipts is immaterial. On the other hand fraudulent production—the production of "illth"—can hardly be counted as adding to the national welfare.

Refinements of Simons's Definition

Simons regarded a broad and objective definition of income as highly important for equity, which in turn he rated as the supreme objective of the tax system. Thus, personal deductions as for contributions and property tax payments were, to say the least, dubious concessions to the taxpayer. And what has since come to be labeled the erosion of the tax base was to him a shocking surrender to special privilege.

Some difficulties of definition are of great interest philosophically but not of much account practically. Simons discussed several of these: for instance, drawing the line between economic and noneconomic activity (as in the case of the hobby farm), psychic income (prestige value of a job), and outlays to improve earning power (education).

Simons's definition of income was broad enough to include gratuities to the donee without a deduction to the donor. This might appear to be double counting, but this was so only because of "the familiar, and disastrous, misconception that personal income is merely a share in some undistributed, separately measurable whole."[16] Faithful to his definition, Simons advocated merger of income, inheritance, and gift taxes. The

14. William W. Hewett, *The Definition of Income and Its Application in Federal Taxation* (Philadelphia: University of Pennsylvania Press, 1925).

15. "Professor Fisher on Income, in the Light of Experience," *American Economic Review* 19 (June 1929): 217–26.

16. Simons, *Personal Income Taxation*, p. 58.

lumpiness of these receipts would be mitigated by generous privileges for averaging.

The reviewer's comment on this proposal is that any good rule (Simons's definition of income) may tolerate a few exceptions. Transfers of property at death are so far removed from the usual run of income (even including capital gains) that to include the two in the same base would, it seems, augment rather than relieve inequities. Simons's proposal is cast in terms of inheritance taxation and it ignores the substantial advantages in taxing estates as such. Among these advantages is the fact that the lump-sum death tax relieves the income tax of the burden of differentiating between property and unfunded income.

Major Issues in Applying the Definition of Income

Simons's definition of income was cast deliberately to include capital accretion, and he applied it to recommend the inclusion of realized capital gains in the tax base without special favor. Parallel treatment would be accorded to capital losses. Constructive realization would catch gains on property passing at death. Averaging would be used to mitigate the problem of lumpiness.

Considerable stress was laid on the fact, not generally appreciated, that the larger part of gains now escape the personal tax system entirely. Combined with the well-developed use of the corporations as a vehicle for personal savings, this means that a large part of the acquisitive economy is entirely immune from the personal tax system. All that is necessary to secure this immunity is to choose the right investments to begin with and hold on. The right investments will be those that feature reinvested earnings instead of dividends. Partly to ease the liquidation problem that attends death transfers Simons developed the idea of allowing taxpayers within limits the option of keeping current with capital gains by paying tax on them when they accrue (with a corresponding adjustment of bases).

Simons took his stand on the ground that we should either abandon progression or face up to the responsibility of taxing all important items that really constitute income. It matters very little that taxation of gains with due recognition of losses might produce little revenue. It isn't yield that is at stake but equity among individuals. It may be noted that Simons largely neglected the principal argument in defense of special treatment for capital gains—namely, that it avoids locking in the taxpayer, preventing exchange of securities. One may well doubt that he would have been much impressed by this defense.

Also vigorously opposed was the retention of tax exemption for interest on state and local bonds. Hitherto this had been opposed mainly on the ground that progression makes sense only when the graduation applies to all one's income. Simons added an attack based on economic grounds; because of the low rate of interest on government bonds resulting from exemption, many who can ill afford to gamble are tempted to invest in more risky securities, including common stocks, whereas others who can and should do the risk-

Henry Simons

bearing for society are persuaded to invest in relatively riskless government bonds.

Also recommended for inclusion in the tax base was income in kind (and without exchange) that the owner derives from an owner-occupied residence.

On the question of income differentiation to favor earned as opposed to funded (property) income Simons argued that the case for such differentiation was weak as long as capital gains were not subject to the full brunt of the tax system. Moreover, property taxes and death taxes already supply some differentiation.

Special depletion allowances were castigated by Simons as an unadulterated racket. Here we may quote a bit more of typical Simonese:

> Legend has it that this was originally a ransom paid by Congress to a gang of prospectors, drillers and option-hawkers who rode right into the Capitol and threatened to shoot the place up if ransom was not paid. The legislation thus attained was explained to Joe Doak as a means of advancing geology.[17]

Treatment of Corporations

Simons gave substantial attention to what is perhaps the hardest problem for the income tax, namely the treatment of corporations, corporate dividends, and undistributed profits. He held firmly to the view that there should be no taxation of business as such, certainly none confined to corporate business. He recognized, however, that some means must be devised to prevent the use of corporations as savings banks free from tax. Accordingly, he was not unsympathetic to the abortive attempt in 1936 to establish an undistributed profits tax though he disliked its impersonal character. Eventually he espoused the idea that the elimination of all special treatment of and favors of capital gains would constitute an adequate means of reaching undistributed profits. Realizing the advantage this would give to corporate as compared with unincorporated business, he proposed also to extend a deduction of reinvested earnings to the latter. The proposal he thought (correctly) would be a handsome bargain for business that it would not fail to accept. He presented his offer (an incentive program) as follows:

> Leave your earnings in the business if you desire. I won't tax you, while you live on any earnings reinvested. In fairness to other taxpayers, you and I must have a comprehensive reckoning sometime (after you are gone or if you get indolent with age, when you retire from ownership participation in the enterprise). Pending that time, however, you may, as it were, borrow from me without interest what

17. Henry C. Simons, *Federal Tax Reform* (Chicago: University of Chicago Press, 1950), p. 96.

you would pay additionally under partnership procedure or the annual appraisal scheme.[18]

Commenting on this audacious program, the reviewer notes that it goes a
long way toward the Fisher proposal to exempt savings from income tax—a
proposal that Simons himself had rejected on the score of its potentialities with
regard to distribution. Time is important in taxation and a concession for a
lifetime is likely to seem to a wage earner (who pays currently on all his receipts) as an unlimited one. The program would mean in effect that the acquisitive economy could escape almost all taxation except for a very severe death
tax. However, it should be added that present practice and all other proposals
for treating corporate income and distributions under the income tax are all
vulnerable to attack on one score or another. No easy and elegant solution of
the problem has thus far been presented. Some defense for the present levy on
corporations has been offered but among other difficulties it accepts too readily the classical view that the incidence of the tax is on stockholders.[19] Some
special impersonal tax on undistributed earnings appears the most rational approach but it is successfully resisted by the business community on the ground
that it would impede the use of internal sources of capital.

Conclusion

The editor of Simons's last book in a prefatory note repeats an opinion
that the important literature on public finance would take up very little space,
a considerable part of which would be occupied by the work of Henry Simons.
This is well-warranted praise.

Of the writers we have so far considered it was Simons who had the highest regard for the direct tax on personal income. He went to the greatest
length in excluding other means as less rational and equitable and economically sound. He had the highest regard for equity in the narrow sense as well as
the broader one of reducing economic inequality. He supplied a basis for supporting progression that must appeal to many as more realistic than that of
the diminishing utility school. He saw that the definition of income and the
exclusions and inclusions therefrom and therein are of vital importance to the
tax.

In the course of this chapter we have recorded some disagreements with
Simons's program and point of view. We might add here that he failed to
develop a satisfactory theory of public expenditure. His views here as far
as they were elaborated, were colored by (what seems to the reviewer to
have been) his considerable bias against government.

But for every shortcoming in Simons's work there are a half dozen

18. Ibid., p. 49.
19. See Richard Goode, *The Corporation Income Tax* (New York: John Wiley and
Sons, 1951).

virtues. For every Utopian scheme or notion there were a half dozen that commend themselves as solid, sensible, and realistic. His work may remain for a long time as the most penetrating and original American contribution in public finance.

PART II
Proponents of Indirect Taxation

9

John Ramsey McCulloch

In the course of the last hundred years in Great Britain and in a much lesser time in the United States, the income tax has become securely lodged as the mainstay of the tax system. Not only that, but the income tax has so long been associated with progression that many have forgotten the alternative of a proportional income tax. A British Royal Commission in 1954 confirmed British commitment to income tax progression with the following statement: "We are satisfied in the present state of public opinion, not merely progressive taxation, but a steep gradient of progressive taxation, is needed in order to conform with the notions of equitable distribution that are widely, almost universally accepted."[1]

That progression and the income tax with which it is associated have ever been so universally accepted, at least in the United States, may be doubted. At any rate this was not always true, and we devote this chapter and the next two chapters to those who contend that a major role in the tax system should be assigned to indirect taxes, that is, to impersonal taxes on expenditure.

Mention has been made of the fact that most of the mercantilist writers held that men should be taxed according to the benefits they receive from the state, and that the measure of such benefits should be expenditure. Sir William Petty had phrased this attractively with his observation that "man is actually and truly rich according to what he eateth, drinketh, weareth, or in any other way really and actually enjoyeth . . ." and should be taxed accordingly.[2]

It is true that internal (i.e. non-tariff) expenditure taxes were not popular in the United States during the era when Alexander Hamilton first sought to impose them. This was probably mainly because of the resentment during the Revolution when the British system had been extended in part to the Colonies. At any rate they led to the celebrated Whiskey Rebellion, and Jefferson

1. Great Britain, Royal Commission on the Taxation of Profits and Income, *Second Report* (London: H.M.S.O., 1954), p. 33.
2. *The Economic Writings of Sir William Petty,* ed. Charles Henry Hull (Cambridge: Harvard University Press, 1894), p. 91.

called them an "infernal system" and his party colleague John Randolph said they were "contrary to the genius of a free people."[3] The British themselves repealed most of their elaborate system during the nineteenth century, extending the repeal to customs as well as internal levies. But circumstances and attitudes toward taxation have undergone many changes since then.

John Ramsey McCulloch (1789–1864), like the founder of modern economics, Adam Smith, was a Scotchman, and he studied at Edinburgh and later lectured at the university there. However, McCulloch never had much association with academic institutions; from 1838 on, he was comptroller of the stationery office until his death. He was an extraordinary compiler, collector, and editor; his *Dictionary of Commerce* (1832) was an important work, and he also published a statistical account of the British Empire and edited works of Smith and Ricardo with biographies appended. His *Principles of Political Economy* was published in 1825 and his *Taxation and the Funding System* in 1845. He is best known in general economics for his support of free trade (tariff for revenue only) and his wages-fund theory, which however was developed out of the work of Ricardo and Malthus. Although his tax recommendations were not very different from those of Smith and Mill, his emphasis was different, and it is this difference which justifies his inclusion in a separate school of thought. He was a man of immense strength and energy and his output was large.

Taxes Paid out of Increased Income

McCulloch made considerable of a contention that taxes (judiciously imposed) might not only be paid out of income, but indeed out of increased income resulting from the stimulation to industry and innovation resulting from taxes. This he thought was the explanation of the historical fact that, notwithstanding heavy taxation, Great Britain during the period 1775 to 1845 had achieved such remarkable economic progress. However, the qualification of "judicious imposition" was stressed; increases must not be too sudden or violent and the degree of levy must stay within moderate limits. "The best taxes, provided they produce the necessary supplies, may, speaking generally, be said to be the lightest, or those of which the pressure is least felt."[4]

More renowned than McCulloch's idea on this matter was his celebrated illustration of the Scottish stills.[5] It seems that before 1786 the duties on spirits

3. Tun Yuan Hu, *The Liquor Tax in the United States, 1791–1947* (New York: Columbia University Graduate School of Business, 1950), pp. 30–32.

4. J. R. McCulloch, *The Taxation and Funding System* (London: Longman, Brown, Green, and Longmans, 1845), p. 6. The idea that taxes could serve as a stimulant, as well as a narcotic, was not new with McCulloch. It is found not infrequently among the mercantilist writers and some of them used it to defend taxes on the poor. The latter would respond to this treatment with improved habits of labor, it was said, and this would be good both for them and the country.

5. Ibid., pp. 151–52.

distilled in Scotland were based on quantities produced. Because of administrative difficulties in this system, the basis of taxation was changed to the size of the still. The rates were adjusted so that at the prevailing productivity of stills the tax burden on producers and the revenue received by the government would not differ greatly from what they had been previously. Almost immediately, however, two ingenious distillers hit upon the idea of lessening the depth and increasing the diameter of the still. In this way a larger surface would be exposed to the fire and the contents could be run off in considerably less time. Applying the idea, the distillers found that they could distill in a few hours what had formerly required a week. Although kept a close secret for a time, the idea eventually became common knowledge and was generally applied by all distillers. In order to maintain its revenue the government was obliged to raise its rate of tax. However, this act of the government provoked further improvement in the construction of stills, which had to be followed by another change in the tax rates. Action and reaction of this sort continued, with the distillers always a step ahead of the government until the productivity of stills had increased 2880 times what it was originally.

This is a neat illustration, but one from which it may not be safe to generalize broadly, since this burst of ingenuity described was associated with an opportunity of avoiding taxes without curtailing output. There never has been any doubt that high taxes create incentives to avoid taxes. But it might be different where there can be no avoidance except to curtail output. It may be worth noting too that there are several means of tax avoidance. One is adjustment in one's private affairs and another is organized effort to procure favorable special amendment to the tax laws. It is only the first of these means of avoidance which is here at issue. Notwithstanding these reservations, McCulloch scored a point in noting that there are at least some exceptions to the rule that taxes are always repressive. Increasing a man's necessary expenditures may as likely as not draw out the extra products to cover the tax. History is full of cases where high taxes and rapid economic growth have been associated.

A Note on Taxes and Output

It is now generally recognized that the supply curve for labor may have a negative slope. In the case of taxes there are usually two conflicting consequences for incentives. In layman's terms, taxes discourage effort because they make alternatives to effort relatively more attractive; they encourage effort because they make more of it necessary to achieve a customary or coveted standard of living. How these two conflicting tendencies balance out in specific situations is not deductively determinable. George Break in a notable study of reactions to high taxes among accountants and lawyers in Great Britain concluded that negative and positive influences fairly well cancelled out.[6] Taxes

6. George F. Break, "Income Taxes and Incentives to Work: An Empirical Study," *American Economic Review* 47 (September 1957): 529-49.

encouraged some to retire earlier than they intended, others later. They encouraged some wives to enter the labor force, others to leave it. It is a matter of common observation that the overworked people in our society are the professional classes, such as the doctors, who may also be the ones who complain most about taxation.

It is a curious fact that the positive effects of taxation on incentives may be observed both in situations where men place a relatively low value on goods as compared to leisure and where the exact opposite is true. The first situation is perhaps more accurately described as one in which people's high regard for goods is pegged at a certain point of achieving necessities. It is said that no wage incentives would appeal to the Indians in early Mexican history. Once having satisfied certain basic needs (corn, beans, cactus juice, and a shack), the Indian preferred to hunt and fish. In certain countries of Africa a poll tax, if it can be collected, is said to stimulate labor. Postponement of retirement in the British context is the opposite case, where men place a low value on leisure as compared with goods. It is a noteworthy fact that the very large influx of working wives into the American labor force has occurred in recent decades of high taxes.

The case of the effect of taxes on saving differs from that on work effort in that tax burdens affect both the capacity and the propensity to save. But there no doubt are cases where people save more both relatively and absolutely because of taxes. This would be the case with a target saver who finds the rate of return on his accumulation reduced by taxes. The case of risk is even more complicated. It is conceded that the full deductibility of losses is important to maintain the balance of odds in a risky venture. Even so, it can be argued plausibly that there is a cut-off point in the acceptable yield of the investments and that taxes (especially corporate taxes) raise this level. But again it is not hard to conceive situations where taxes will encourage risk-taking. For instance a taxpayer whose marginal dollars have ceased to have much value for him because of taxes or whatnot may gamble very freely for sport.

Convenience versus Equity

McCulloch's emphasis upon convenience as against equity becomes apparent early in his book where he cites Adam Smith's four canons and stresses the latter three (certainty, convenience, and economy), describing equity as a matter of secondary importance. Equity is entitled to some weight in direct taxation, but he thought direct taxation should be used sparingly. "It is the business of the legislator to look at the practical influence of different taxes and to resort in preference to those by which the revenue may be raised with least inconvenience."[7]

7. McCulloch, *Taxation and Funding System*, p. 10.

John Ramsey McCulloch

Recalling the views of previous writers, we can see here a sharp issue making its appearance. It is an issue between what may be called the rationalists and what we shall term without prejudice the opportunists.

Selective Sales Tax

The type of levy that appealed most to McCulloch was what in our day we would call a selective sales tax. He bowed to the prevailing view of his time to agree that taxes on necessities should be imposed with great caution and restraint. He made the usual exception for goods consumed by the poor, but not essential to their maintenance. And he showed some sympathy for the mercantilist view that the repeal of indirect taxes might deprive the poor of the incentives which make the lower classes industrious.

"Indirect taxes have with few exceptions been the great favorites both of princes and subjects; and there are very sufficient reasons for the preference."[8] One of the reasons is the facility and cheapness with which such taxes can be collected. Another is their optional character—if anyone complains about being overburdened by taxes of this sort, he can be told that his burden is his own fault. A third support for consumption taxes is their tendency to foster saving. If misers avoid these taxes, they do so by adding to the store of capital, and this will add to the productivity and wealth of the nation. It will hardly lead to excessive personal accumulation; one generation of misers rarely follows another. We can depend upon the profligate sons of the miserly rich to undo the frugality of the fathers.

McCulloch considered some of the objections of his preferred type of levy and dismissed them as either invalid or attributable to excessive rates. Thus, he noted the allegation that such taxes "alter the distribution of capital and industry and force them into less advantageous channels."[9] McCulloch met the point with the observation that so far as producers' interests are concerned, redistribution of capital would restore normal profits in industries subject to special tax. The subtler loss of consumers who shift their pattern of consumption to avoid tax escaped him. The temptation to smuggle (a prevalent practice which was conceded to be a considerable scandal) could be avoided by moderation in rates. The phenomenon of pyramiding was noted, but McCulloch was of the opinion that other writers had exaggerated its importance.

Taxes on liquor and tobacco appealed to McCulloch as specially qualified exhibitors of the above-mentioned virtues of consumption taxes. In addition, he approved of their sumptuary qualifications. However, he went beyond these to approve taxes on sugar, bricks, glass, paper, soap, and vinegar. These were all subjects for the extensive British consumption tax system of his day. Levies on salt and candles had been repealed, and McCulloch did not suggest their revival.

8. Ibid., p. 148.
9. Ibid., p. 153.

Proponents of Indirect Taxation

Of the several points listed above, we may single out the alleged optional feature of consumption taxes for special comment. It was this feature apparently that most appealed to McCulloch. Had he noted the sacrifices involved in forsaking preferences, he might have lost some of his confidence in the persuasiveness of the point. Another British author, Edwin Cannon, suggested years later that a man who goes two miles out of his way to avoid a toll bridge might be more benefited by the freeing of the bridge than most men who paid the toll.[10]

It has long been noted that compulsion is the unique, the unpopular, and perhaps the evil feature of taxation. To diminish its degree would seem accordingly to be highly advantageous. If in the democratic process some minority folk find themselves in a position where government indulges in expenditures they do not like, they would be better satisfied if they had some choice about participating in the contribution. The direct way to accomplish this is to charge a fee for use of the proposed facility. But this ignores the indirect benefits of the project, which, say the proponents, will be shared by everybody. Private giving also presumably involves no onus of compulsion. Next, less compulsion would occur, according to McCulloch, where the project is paid for by indirect taxes. This may not appeal to a rationalist, who sees only that if all men share in the indivisible benefits of government, all should help pay for them (no options).

One advantage of a degree of option in taxes is that it reduces opposition to taxation and to the expansion of governmental services. Here the appeal may be to the left, where there has long been some frustration over the handicaps of public service in competing with private outlays.

It should be added that the difference among taxes in terms of compulsion is altogether a matter of degree. Income taxes can be avoided too, especially if they allow full deduction of contributions to social causes. Almost any tax on industry and thrift would not reach large taxpayers if they would but adopt the way of life of the medieval monk. Even the poll tax can be avoided by committing suicide, and while this might bring on a death tax, there are also choices that will get around this latter levy.

One may doubt too that any tax is as coercive as some critics argue. If representative government works, at least 51 percent of the people must support it, and for them the tax is not coercive. For many others some degree of acquiescence may be expected; they bow to majority opinion in this case as they do in most private organizations without renouncing their membership.

Direct Levies

Curiously McCulloch's tolerance of inequity in indirect taxation was not paralleled by a similar easy standard for direct taxation. Thus he argued against

10. Quoted by E. R. A. Seligman, *The Shifting and Incidence of Taxation,* 4th ed. (New York: Columbia University Press, 1921), p. 13.

the income tax on the ground that a dollar of income from professional services represents much less capacity than one from property. But any attempt to make a distinction that would recognize such differences would make the income tax too complicated.

As one would expect, McCulloch's major argument against direct taxes was on the score of administrative difficulties. Property taxes confronted an impossible task of evaluation; income taxes were plagued by inaccessibility of required information. It is not and never will be possible to assess with tolerable precision the income of farmers, manufacturers, dealers of all sorts, and professional men. Self-assessment in their case can mean only "a bounty on perjury and fraud," plus an obnoxious inquisitorial invasion of the citizen's privileges of privacy. Thus, income taxes, though theoretically equal and in accord with Utopian ideals, must prove as applied in this world most unequal and impractical.

Like Mill and Smith, McCulloch expressed a strong preference among direct taxes for a house tax. Here again the appeal lay in the element of choice. Those who felt that the house tax was getting burdensome need only move to a cheaper house. The reviewer notes that in our day McCulloch's option as to houses is proving distasteful to older people.

Progression

McCulloch had no use for progression and the best known passages in his book are those with which he denounced this institution. To quote a few of them:

> No tax on income can be just unless it leaves individuals in the same relative condition in which it found them.

> Let it not be supposed that the principle of graduation may be carried to a certain extent, and then stopped.

> Graduation is not an evil to be paltered with. Adopt it and you will effectively paralyze industry and check accumulation, at the same time that any man who has any property will hasten, by carrying it out of the country, to protect it from confiscation. The savages described by Montesquieu, who to get at the fruit cut down the tree, are about as good financiers as the advocates of this sort of taxes. Wherever they are introduced security is at an end. Even if taxes on income were otherwise unexceptionable, the adoption of graduation would make them about the very worst that could be devised. The moment you abandon, in the framing of such taxes, the cardinal principle of exacting the same proportion of their income or of their property, you are at sea without rudder or compass, and there is no amount of injustice and folly you may not commit.[11]

11. J. R. McCulloch, *Taxation and Funding System*, pp. 141, 142, 142–43.

Proponents of Indirect Taxation

Except for one observation in general and some analysis of the leave-them-as-you-find-them proposition, we shall pass by these eloquent and provocative passages. The observation is that authors like McCulloch made progression look so ominous that it is a wonder that men even in the twentieth century ever had the temerity to try it.

The leave-them-as-you-find-them rule, which was not original with McCulloch,[12] might seem to take on some sort of sanction from the natural order. But this is not self-evident and presumes some agreement concerning the distribution of benefits from government. It will be observed that when rich and poor buy the same bundle of goods privately, the rule doesn't hold and the poor become relatively poorer.

The leave-them-as-you-find-them rule would hardly appeal to one who was dissatisfied with the distribution of income before taxes. Must it be accepted by one who has no quarrel with such distribution? We have considered this issue before and have arrived at a negative answer. In the payment for social services in lieu of private services, one has to compare (however roughly) the social importance of everything: for instance, A's second automobile, B's shirt, the public school, and a new army tank. In doing so, he could conclude that the new tank was more essential than A's automobile, but not as important (socially) as B's shirt. And he might find that progressive taxation plus public spending for the tank is the only available means to implement this judgment. This need imply no discontent with A's retention of the automobile were there no collective need for the tank.

Conclusion

McCulloch's contribution to tax literature was neither very original nor very profound. But nowhere else in the annals can one find the case for the opportunistic approach to taxation (including the preference for indirect taxes and the repugnance for progression) so confidently and uncompromisingly propounded. The exception perhaps is Harley Lutz, whose reactions to the tax problem are sharply reminiscent of McCulloch. To his work we now turn.

---

12. Sir William Petty has argued that a proportional tax would be relatively burdenless, because relative wealth would not be changed. This view was most eloquently propounded by William Pitt in his original proposal of an income tax in 1798: "What does the new tax do? Are they not left in relation to each other precisely as they were before? The tax creates no new inequality. The justice or injustice remain precisely as they were. To complain of this inequality is to complain of the constitution of society. To attempt to remedy it, would be to follow the example of that daring rabble of legislators in another country . . . To think of taxing two species of income in a different ratio, would be to attempt what the nature of society will not admit." Quoted in E. R. A. Seligman, *The Income Tax* (New York: Macmillan Co., 1911), pp. 74–75.

10

Lutz and Galbraith

Strange Bedfellows

Harley L. Lutz

Harley L. Lutz, a contemporary American economist, received his doctorate at Harvard in 1914. His dissertation, *The State Tax Commission,* published by the Harvard Press in 1918, was awarded a David A. Wells prize. Dr. Lutz by then had become professor of economics at Oberlin College (1909–23). From Oberlin he went to Stanford University, where he remained until 1928. The first edition of his textbook, *Public Finance,* appeared in 1924. His final academic post was at Princeton, where he remained from 1928 until his retirement in 1937. He then became consulting economist for the National Association of Manufacturers. Lutz's earlier views, presented in successive editions of his textbook, could be described as somewhere near the center of the spectrum, but he was sadly disillusioned by the New Deal and became a sharp critic of existing tax practices. A series of his lectures at Stanford University was published in 1939 as *The Business Man's Stake in Government Finance.* Before his retirement at Princeton he contributed a series of articles to the *Tax Review;* these were subsequently reprinted in a volume entitled *Guideposts to a Free Economy* (1945). Some of the following is also gleaned from many articles which he has written over the years.

Criticism of Income Taxation

"Federal taxation of income made possible by the 16th amendment," he wrote in 1941, "had long been the dream of tax reformers. The system of taxation that has developed under this amendment is today regarded, by many, as perfection in a world of imperfect taxes. To criticize it, except in the most friendly and favorable way, is to lay hands on the Ark of the Covenant."[1]

Lutz proceeded without any inhibitions on this score. "It has been

1. Harley L. Lutz, "Some Errors and Fallacies of Taxation as Exemplified by the Federal Income Tax," *Proceedings of the National Tax Association Conference, 1941,* p. 355.

assumed . . . from the beginning," he said, "that the only proper way of applying the 16th amendment is to levy on some vague, but emotionally satisfactory tax base called net income."[2] The base, he thought, was unsatisfactory because among other reasons it allowed insufficiently for business losses, for the personal expenses of the taxpayer associated with personal income, for the difference in time patterns of income flow. In addition, there was too much delay in applying the tax. Moreover, the income tax is inherently inquisitorial in nature and susceptible to various forms of blackmail.

On Progression

In his later work Lutz turned against progressive taxation with vehemence. His arguments here are singularly reminiscent of McCulloch. First, there is the matter of arbitrariness:

> Here it is sufficient to point out that no one knows for certain just how much faster so-called ability increases as income rises, if at all. Therefore, there is no just or progressive tax rate scale. Every such scale is the product of guesswork and of political and fiscal expediency. And where expediency is the basis of policy, it is easy to lapse into injustice.[3]

On further reflection Lutz sees even proportional taxation as quite arbitrary and unfair:

> . . . the basis of our support of the workers in the private sector of our economy is the system of prices. Per unit, a given item is sold to all and sundry at the same price per unit. No one is required to fill out Form 1040 to enable a merchant to determine how much to charge him for bread or shoes or coal.
> Why should anyone be forced to contribute to the support of the government on a basis different from that on which he contributes to the support of other parts of the economy?[4]

The passage is revealing. It is true that all taxation is more or less arbitrary; no definitive pattern is prescribed either by natural law or scientific analysis. Following the market pattern of the private economy is no less arbitrary than its alternatives. It would merely cope with uncertainties by resolving all the doubts in favor of the wealthy.

Principal argument against progression (again following McCulloch) is that the latter encroaches upon potential capital and injures incentive. Referring specifically to the spectacular development of the Ford Motor Company, largely out of untaxed undistributed profits, he offers this effective

2. Ibid.
3. Harley L. Lutz, *Guideposts to a Free Economy* (New York: McGraw-Hill Book Co., 1945), p. 70.
4. Lutz, "Some Errors," p. 370.

Lutz and Galbraith

warning, calculated to send chills down the backs of the perplexed American voter:

> The American people face a serious choice here, one that involves their destiny as certainly as any foreign battlefield or postwar peace conference. Concretely and in terms of an historical parallel, it is a choice between the Ford fortune and the Ford automobile. If they shall decide that there shall be no more fortunes, they will also thereby decide that there shall be no commodities of mass comfort and enjoyment other than those now known. A few large fortunes would appear to be a small price to pay to gain the full benefit of all the creative and productive capacity that can be stimulated most efficiently and most certainly by allowing those who succeed to keep the profits of their success.[5]

The reviewer notes that the above statement is too unguarded to pass for more than propaganda. Observation does not support the contention that innovation is dependent upon large fortunes or that big aggregations of capital cannot survive progressive taxation. Since free enterprise encountered this alleged bolt of lightning, there have been rather impressive developments in both respects.

Going beyond McCulloch, Lutz observed that progressive taxation is a tenet of communism or socialism, and while not all of its proponents can be accused of seeking to weaken the free enterprise system for the socialist kill, the others unwittingly play into the hands of the revolutionaries.[6]

The reviewer notes that no doubt there have been some ties of sympathy between some egalitarians and some socialists. But the two interests appear to overlap surprisingly little. Socialists have been principally interested in a new organization of production rather than radical changes in distribution via taxation. It would be at least as plausible to argue that redistribution lessens the likelihood of other revolution as the reverse. The Russian experience involved some experimentation with egalitarianism, but the latter was rejected as impractical and not essential to the Socialist ideal.

Consumption Taxes

Dr. Lutz is a proponent of excise taxation and prefers a general to a special (selective) excise system. The case against special excises, he says, lies in their discriminatory character. Excepting liquor and tobacco, there is no case for singling out certain commodities as luxuries and placing a special burden on them and/or their producers.

This is persuasive, but the reviewer is unable to accept the proposition that there are no differences in terms of social significance between food, fuel, and

5. Lutz, *Guideposts,* p. 82.
6. Ibid., p. 77.

utility clothing on the one hand, and cameras, mechanical refrigerators, and jewelry on the other. The classical economists may have drawn these distinctions for the wrong reasons, but their conclusion was nonetheless valid. It is true that distinctions of this sort are hard to make and their validity cannot be verified. This is also true of the hundred and one other decisions that attend a typical budget.

Lutz submits several interesting arguments for a general federal sales tax, among them the following: A general sales tax would add diversity to the tax system. "A combination of sales and income taxes would be like carrying a load on both shoulders instead of one."[7] There are limits to the successful application of the income tax; the consumption tax is better adapted to reach a broader base.

We have commented before on the diversity aspect of taxation. The reviewer would make no case for a single tax, but he also is skeptical about adding members to the tax system on no stronger ground than that they add numbers and variety to the system. It can be recalled in this connection that all taxes, with some qualifications, come out of the same stream—namely income.

As to the regressivity of consumption taxes, Lutz argues that "the same hard fact is encountered in the whole system of market prices. . . . In view of the general acceptance of the market prices system, which is thoroughly regressive in the sense this term is now used, the objection to a tax which would constitute so small a fraction of the grand total of consumer spending, on the ground that it is regressive, is a case of swallowing the camel but straining at the gnat."[8]

As to the effect of consumption taxes on resource allocation, "It would appear that, contrary to the accepted notions, taxes on consumption will have less effect on the operation of the economy as a whole than taxes which impair the nation's capacity to enlarge the capital fund."[9]

A manufacturers' tax is preferred to a retail tax because the former would be cheaper to administer and conflict less with the tax systems of the states. Pyramiding would be greater in the case of the manufacturers' levy; but distributive business is intensely competitive, and this should check the tendency to add to the tax as it is passed along.

Taxation for Non-fiscal Purposes

One idea in Professor Lutz's philosophy, and this is of long standing, holds that taxation should not be used for non-fiscal purposes. Thus, in his text he

7. Ibid., p. 101.
8. "The Place and Role of Consumption Taxes in the Federal Tax Structure," *Federal Tax Policy for Growth and Stability* (Washington, D.C.: Joint Committee on the Economic Report, 1955), p. 569.
9. Harley L. Lutz, *The Businessman's Stake in Government Finance* (Stanford: Graduate School of Business, Stanford University, 1939), p. 12.

quotes with approval the British tax economist, C. F. Bastable: "To mix up with one very important objective another different and perhaps incompatible one is to run the risk of failing in both."[10]

The reviewer would inquire how, if there is no objective standard of tax equity, one could possibly avoid gauging taxes by their effects even if he wanted to do so. Nevertheless, there is an element of validity in Lutz's position. Many critics accept the view that we have gone too far in using the tax laws, particularly the income tax law, to serve too many objectives. A safe conclusion is that use of the tax system for non-fiscal purposes should carry a considerable burden of proof; such relief should be reserved for important objectives, that clearly can be achieved most effectively through the tax mechanism.

In summary, we are indebted to Dr. Lutz for a clearly defined, vigorous, and unambiguous point of view featuring consumption taxes and opposing trends toward single progressive taxation of income and wealth. Almost alone among the critics he makes it clear that proportional taxation is subject to the same limitations as progressive taxation. This is the cardinal point that Blum and Kalven (see chap. 6, above) overlooked. Lutz is regarded as a spokesman for highly conservative interests. But other people who not by any stretch would qualify for the conservative label arrive for quite different reasons at some of the same conclusions about direct (sales) taxes. To one of these we shall now turn our attention.

John Kenneth Galbraith

The third representative in our so-called opportunistic school of thought is also a contemporary—John Kenneth Galbraith of Harvard University. Galbraith was originally from Canada and got his bachelor's degree from the University of Toronto in 1931. His advanced degrees were from the University of California (doctorate, 1934). He was instructor and tutor at Harvard from 1934 to 1939 and assistant professor at Princeton from 1939 to 1942. He studied abroad at Cambridge, England, during the year 1937–38. He served as deputy administrator of O.P.A. during World War II and on the board of editors of *Fortune* magazine from 1943 to 1948. In 1948 he returned to Harvard, and since then he has given birth to a series of highly provocative and widely read books, including: *American Capitalism: The Concept of Countervailing Power* (1952), *Economics and the Art of Controversy* (1955), *The Affluent Society* (1958), and *The New Industrial State* (1967). Whatever may be said of his ideas, the artistry and style of his work is admired by all critics. Moreover, his books are an example of the beneficent Great Debate concerning matters of economic policy and philosophy and of which we have had occasion to speak before. Their influence has been pervasive and profound.

10. Harley L. Lutz, *Public Finance,* 2d. ed. (New York: D. Appleton and Co., 1929), p. 313; the original is found in C. F. Bastable, *Public Finance* (London: Macmillan and Co., 1927), p. 336.

In the first of these books Galbraith assumed the role of institutional economist and examined a world which defies most of the rules of the classical
economists and yet works—in recent years "quite brilliantly." [11] He found the
answer in "countervailing power"; huge aggregations of capital, labor and government are arrayed against each other to maintain an equilibrium. In the second book mentioned above, Galbraith dealt with the question How seriously
are Americans divided on economic matters? His answer was, Hardly serious
enough to make life interesting. And the trend is away from the extremes,
drawing more and more Americans into the middle. One of the matters on
which consensus has broadened is the progressive income tax. Extremists continue to rail against this and other measures espoused by the middle; one reason
is that they see little hope for the broad acceptance of their point of view. [12]

Although none of Galbraith's works give more than passing attention to
taxation, he is included here because of his support of the sales tax on especially interesting grounds. No one will deny, least of all the parties involved, that
H. Lutz and J. K. Galbraith make strange bedfellows.

The Income Tax

It is not to be inferred that because Galbraith is included in our present
series he must be opposed to the progressive income tax, offering the sales tax
as a substitute. On the contrary, in his *American Capitalism* he praises the income tax for its contribution to economic stability (built-in flexibility). Moreover, he regards the tax as equally valuable in terms of political stability; here
it makes high incomes respectable and appeases the envy of the dispossessed.
"Conservatives should build a statue to it and to its inspired progenitor, President William Howard Taft." [13]

But for Galbraith the progressive income tax is not worth much attention
because the main battle for it has been fought and won. This is evident from
the high stability of the federal tax system in recent years notwithstanding
changes of parties in power. And the income tax is not available for much expansion in public revenue. It is held in deadlock by a balance of forces: conservatives wouldn't dare to make it more productive at the expense of its progressivity, and liberals wouldn't want to do so. Moreover, the income tax is ir-
retrievably associated with acrimonious debates about inequality and socialism,
now irrelevant. Especially at the state and local level, this type of levy may
not for a variety of reasons be available to yield the large additional sums still
needed to give the public services their due. Sales taxes, he argues, may have
the advantage of greater political palatability.

11. John Kenneth Galbraith, *American Capitalism: The Concept of Countervailing
Power* (Boston: Houghton Mifflin Co., 1952), p. 1.
12. John K. Galbraith, *Economics and the Art of Controversy* (New Brunswick:
Rutgers University Press, 1955).
13. Galbraith, *American Capitalism,* p. 188.

Sales Tax

The most striking opportunity for improvement in our current situation, says Galbraith in *The Affluent Society,* is in expanding public services—particularly education. Public services occupy a large domain unsuited (because of indirect benefits) for production and exchange in the private economy. They lag because they somehow carry the taint of social revolution—they are still associated with the fears engendered by Karl Marx. Actually these services and their expansion pose no threat to the private economic system. "Clearly the competition between public and private services, apart from any question of the satisfaction they render, is an unequal one." [14]

This brings us to Galbraith's case for the sales tax: "The community is affluent in privately produced goods. It is poor in public services. The obvious solution is to tax the former to provide the latter—by making private goods more expensive public goods are made more abundant." [15] Even if such a tax might seem to aggravate poverty, this is an illusion because the cure for the kind of poverty which now exists is richer educational opportunity. The left favors income taxes and the right, sales taxes; if the latter is willing to accept higher taxes on condition that it name the species to be employed, the left should accede to the bargain since its stake in the public services outweighs that in the mode of taxation.

Criticism and Conclusion

Galbraith's books in the reviewer's opinion perform the much needed service of analyzing the new environment in which the tax systems of highly developed Western economies must be appraised. His success in this regard serves to remind us that tax institutions and even tax principles have to be gauged in terms of the conditions of time and place. It could be that the principles that once seemed eminently rational and persuasive are now invalid or irrelevant. Protection of a minimum, for instance, regarded as essential by Smith and Mill, is a less compelling matter under conditions of widespread abundance and many public services ubiquitously enjoyed. Particularly where, for various reasons, further development of the income tax is an unavailable alternative, sales taxes will often appear, even to those who do not like them, as preferable to gross inadequacies in the public economy.

There are, however, reservations to be recorded:

1. The sales tax ignores the social interest in minimum private spending. Private goods and public goods are complementary—an expensive school for poorly nourished children is bad distribution of resources. Many a good teacher

14. John Kenneth Galbraith, *The Affluent Society* (Boston: Houghton Mifflin Co., 1958), p. 137.

15. Leo Word, "The We Can't Afford It Chant," quoted in the *Congressional Record*, February 28, 1961, p. 2610.

in an excellent school has been frustrated by pupils with a poor home environment. The latter is not entirely a matter of poverty, but one can hardly doubt that an overtight budget is responsible for much of the problem. The notion that education will take under these circumstances and defeat poverty in the next generation, requires a good deal of faith.

2. Not only do many sales taxes provide a regressive distribution of the tax load without a minimum exemption; in addition they do a very rough job of rationing the tax load among equals. They hunt for revenue with a shotgun rather than a rifle. With taxation taking so large a share of everyone's earnings, should we not insist on higher, rather than accept lower, standards of rationality in its distribution?

Most versions of the opportunistic approach to taxation carry the theme that the end justifies the means. The public lottery is a fairly extreme case of this sort. The Marxians, many of them, take the greatest liberties with this reasoning. Stalin is said to have begun his distinguished career by robbing banks and caravans for the cause of the Communist Party. The reviewer suspects that some of his own colleagues believe so fervently in the cause of education that they would go nearly that far.

One should be wary of the thesis that the end never justifies the means. It all depends on the circumstances—one of which is the importance of the end and another the degree to which the means is unconscionable. But a good end never justifies a poor means if there is a better one at hand.

PART III
*Proponents of a Personal
Spendings Tax*

11

Fisher, Vickrey, and Kaldor

If one concedes that ability to pay, on some definition, should be the criterion of tax distribution, that direct taxation is the proper means of applying this standard, and that progression in the application of direct taxation is desirable, one is still not obliged to accept income (or wealth) as the proper or best tax base. Expenditure is also a possible measure, and its support for such a role has a long history and a recent revival of interest. Included in the roster of its supporters (at least in terms of an ideal) are the celebrated names of John Stuart Mill, Alfred Marshall, A. C. Pigou, and Irving Fisher.

One can conceive a graduated expenditure tax as a progressive income tax with current saving exempt from the tax base. However, to make the proposal acceptable, expenditure from past saving must also be included; otherwise one could defeat the tax by always spending last year's income.

We have dealt in an earlier chapter with the general ideas concerning taxation entertained and presented by John Stuart Mill. We there suggested that his ideas were sufficiently eclectic to give him a place in several of the schools of tax philosophy into which we here classify the English and American writers on taxation. In Mill's view the tax on savings upsets the neutrality of the income tax and violates the canon of equity.[1] We shall encounter this analysis in one form or another in all the proponents of the expenditure tax, and we shall have occasion to discuss it later.

Pigou followed Mill in the view that the income tax is prejudicial to saving and added that it gives less than proper weight to the social interest in accumulation. He agreed with Mill that an expenditure tax would encounter insuperable administrative difficulty. However, Pigou entertained the idea that progression might be applied to expenditure in much the same way that it is now applied to general income.

Although the interest in a spendings tax in the United States as well as Great Britain has been principally academic, there have been several occasions

---

1. John Stuart Mill, *Principles of Political Economy* (London: Longmans, Green, and Co., 1919), bk. 5, chap. 2, sec. 4, pp. 813–14.

in the United States where it knocked on the door of practical affairs. The idea was favored by Dr. T. S. Adams while he was tax advisor to the Treasury, and a legislative proposal of this sort was introduced by Congressman Ogden L. Mills after World War I. During World War II when controlling inflation was a grievous problem, and Congress and the Treasury were deadlocked over the issue of a sales tax versus further increase in the income tax, or neither, the Treasury startled the Senate Finance Committee with a spendings tax proposal. The bewildered committee and the newspapers found it difficult to classify this tax as a sales tax, or an income tax, or neither. Under the circumstances of the proposal, the tax could be defended not only as a revenue producer but also as an overall rationing device. It would tell the citizen in effect that he might spend according to his preference, but if he spent too much he would be fined for it. The proposal was not warmly received, however, and it has not been revived.

Irving Fisher

The notion that net income should be defined to exclude savings has long been associated with the name of the American economist Irving Fisher (1867–1947). Fisher received all of his degrees at Yale, the doctorate in 1891. His first position, also at Yale, was assistant professor of mathematics but he turned to economics in 1895. He is said to have been the first competent American mathematical economist. During 1893 and 1894 he studied in Paris and Berlin. His works were numerous, among them two on mathematics and several on health matters and prohibition. His first noteworthy book in economics was *The Nature of Capital and Interest* (1906); it was followed by several other books on interest and money. His interest in tax matters was incidental to his interest in the nature of income, but he did write a book entitled *Constructive Income Taxation* (1942) and several articles on the proper conception of the income tax base.

Definition of Income

Fisher was confident that his exposition of the nature of income would clear up a host of ambiguities associated with that subject and leave no room at all for disagreement and misunderstanding. He approached the matter from the standpoint of accounting—"the ordinary bookkeeper's art of debiting and crediting." The total net income from a given source is the net sum derived by adding together the value of its services and disservices. In double-entry bookkeeping, savings (or reinvestments) are a negative not a positive item, offsets to income rather than income. Capital gains, whether or not realized, are a capital item until they are spent. Similarly, depreciation is not outgo; it is only a sort of accrual for repairs which becomes negative when an outlay is made for them.

As a clinching example, Fisher suggests three brothers, each of whom inherits $100,000.[2] The first invests this in an annuity which will yield him $5,000 in perpetuity and spends the receipts annually. The second lets the income accumulate for fourteen years (saves and reinvests $5,000 annually during this period), at which time it will have doubled its value and he can and does enjoy a $10,000 income thereafter. The third, being of the spendthrift type, draws $20,000 per year for (nearly) six years and reinvests nothing. Suppose a 10 percent income tax on the three brothers. Each will bear the same burden in terms of capitalized value of tax *if* the assessment is timed according to spending. That is, $10,000 is the sum in present cash which is equal to $500 a year forever, to $1,000 per year beginning fourteen years hence, and to $2,000 per year for six years. The income tax as ordinarily calculated gives very different results. For instance, the capitalized value of the burden on the second brother (the saver) turns out to be $17,140. "Such a system of taxation is clearly unjust, not to say that it discourages the saver, while it encourages the spendthrift."[3]

It is a neat illustration, but in the reviewer's opinion it only proves what no one would deny, namely, that if income is consumption, then the saver should not be taxed until he consumes. If income is net receipts the saver should pay more because he enhances his income. Any practice of the economic virtues leads to the same results. Let us restate the issue in simpler terms: A and B each earn $2,000 in 1970 and A saves the money while B spends. In 1971 each again earns $2,000, but A has an increment of $100 in interest; B also has an increment of $100 from extra labor (working overtime). Suppose also that the income tax falls equally on the two in the years when the money comes in. Has A any reason to complain? Each pays on $4,100, which is what he received and spent. The choice of timing in expenditures is the taxpayer's. One sacrifices in the postponement of consumption, the other in extra effort. Society gains capital in one case, labor in the other. Is there more to this than the simple fact that anyone who chooses to enlarge his income and makes an extra sacrifice to this end must share his reward with the government? As to psychic rewards, who is to say that current spending yields more satisfaction than postponement? It is true as Mill pointed out that A's interest would be greater if he could save and invest without tax. But would not this concession give an unneutral advantage to A's pattern of disposition as compared with B's? The answer is surely "yes" if the *power* of disposition (the availability of choice) is the essence of income. Fisher's illustration (and Mill's) only proves what is obvious from their initial assumptions.

2. Irving Fisher, *The Income Concept in the Light of Experience,* English reprint [New Haven? 1927?], pp. 12–13; originally in volume 3 of the *Wieser Festschrift, Die Wirts* [c] *haft* [s] *theorie der Gegenwart* (Vienna, 1927).

3. Ibid., p. 13.

Proponents of a Personal Spendings Tax

Nature of a Spendings Tax

"Theoretically," said Fisher, "a meticulous income tax should pursue its victim to the dining table and take toll from each mouthful, and should go with him to the theater and tax every laugh."[4] (Presumably also if the meal turns out badly or the theatre performance does not please, he should get a discount.) But since measurability is essential for practical taxation, we may settle for a system that would apply a strict method of bookkeeping balances to all the taxpayer's transactions. This would, for Fisher, leave consumption of the value of end product (or previous accumulation) as the basis for tax. Consumer's capital would constitute a special problem: a house that the tax-payer owns and uses may be written off in installments; in the case of furniture we might for convenience levy the tax at the time of purchase. Fisher appears at one time to have expressed skepticism concerning the application to society of the same standards of appraisal as regards saving that one would apply to individuals, but he had no Keynesian fears that unlimited accumulation might exceed opportunities for investment. Excessive accumulation would be checked by reduction in the interest rate.[5]

A sensible conclusion in the reviewer's opinion might hold that the benefit of much saving in a mature economy is not so well established as to warrant tax discrimination. If saving needs encouragement there are other means to this end than tax subsidy. But this gets us back again to the fundamental issue of whether the income tax is really unneutral as between saving and spending.

In summary, Irving Fisher was the first to explore fully the theoretical implications of including saving in the concept of income for tax purposes. He was the first to devote a full book to the subject and (until Kaldor) the most confident that he had the correct answer to the income tax problem in terms both of equity and economic effects. His single-tracked approach posed the issue sharply and it proved highly provocative to many critics. It is as well for the issue perhaps that he was completely myopic to the very great deal that is to be said on the other side of his proposals.

William Vickrey

William Vickrey (1914-   ) received his undergraduate degree at Yale, where he undoubtedly encountered Irving Fisher with whose career his own has been in some respects comparable. During World War II he was on the Treasury's tax research staff and he had some part in the abortive attempt to launch a wartime spendings tax. His doctoral dissertation, *Agenda for Progressive Taxation,* was published in 1947. It is a much quoted book and along with Simons's earlier study, constitutes a highwater mark in originality among doctor's dissertations. Vickrey received his doctorate from

5. See Joseph Dorfman, *The Economic Mind in American Civilization,* (New York: Viking Press, 1949), 3: 370.

Columbia University in 1947 and has been a member of its staff since that time.

Cumulative Averaging

It should be said for the record that the *Agenda* was not primarily about the spendings tax, nor was that tax endorsed by Vickrey for anything like an exclusive role. A reform proposal that has come to be most closely associated with Vickrey's name is that of life-time cumulative averaging of income for the income tax base. There had been many averaging proposals in the literature before Vickrey, but his was no doubt the most ambitious. To begin with, as the term for his proposal suggests, he aimed at a very long period, ideally from the taxpayer's age of maturity until his death. Then there is the cumulative feature. The idea here was to add each year's income plus interest on previously paid taxes to a cumulative total and to calculate a tax on this sum from which would be deducted taxes previously paid plus interest to give the current amount due.[6] Opening and closing inventories of assets would give a capital-gains figure for the final accounting. This and the interest factor aim at much more than a simple mitigation of the harshness in applying graduated rates to fluctuating income. They aim to defeat the many gimmicks of tax postponement such as the reinvestment of corporate earnings and tax-postponement pension plans. And of course, they aim to solve the capital-gains problem. In short, this is a major effort to solve all the problems of timing in income taxation at one stroke.

Taxpayers with the same lifetime earnings over the same length of life would pay the same tax in terms of the present value of tax payments. Note that the interest factor is not applied to income itself. A taxpayer who receives most of his income in the early years of his life, other things being equal, is not penalized on that account even though early enjoyment may be thought to give him an advantage. The penalty is reserved for the taxpayer who earns early and pays late.

Note also that taxes as well as income are cumulated. The system automatically recalculates the tax of previous years and allows the taxpayer in a bad year to anticipate a refund. This in turn supports the claim that the system is countercyclical.

Vickrey's ingenious proposal, in spite of its undoubted merits, ranks high on the list of proposals too subtle and elaborate for Congress, even if the latter were disposed to accept that part of the program which calls for the full-tax

6. Thus if A in his first year of averaging has a $5,000 income and pays $1,000 in tax, he will carry forward to his second year (assuming interest at 5 percent) $5,050 of income and $1,050 of taxes. Note that the interest factor is added to both the income and tax side of the account. Early payment of tax being credited with interest makes the tax equivalent to an investment, and the taxpayer earns on it in addition to his other income.

treatment of capital gains. Moreover, some critics have been skeptical of trying to reckon taxpaying capacity on the whole of one's lifetime experience. They argue for a more limited period on which taxpayers generally base their behavior. Finally, all averaging schemes, especially the more ambitious ones, are embarrassed by the imputed value of leisure, not recognized by the income tax.

If Mrs. A earns $5,000 every year and Mrs. B earns $10,000 every other year because she voluntarily moves in and out of the labor force, are the two to be treated as equal? If Mr. C and Mr. D each have the same lifetime earnings, but C retired at the age of fifty-five and D continued to work until he was seventy years old, should they, over the years, pay the same taxes? Actually, lifetime cumulative averaging would give the better break to C, who earned more of his income and paid more taxes earlier than D.

Vickrey, above all authors in the reviewer's annal, was sharply aware of the problems of timing in taxation and he extended his attention to the death tax as well as the income tax, here proposing devices similar to his lifetime averaging but even more formidable. For a simpler reform he first proposed adjusting the tax according to the age differential between the heir and the deceased. This would favor early giving and penalize postponement devices, such as the skip-a-generation trust, which have long plagued the critics.

Spendings Tax

The author agrees with Mill and Fisher that the present tax system is unneutral as between spending and saving. It "disturbs the natural exchange ratio between present and future consumption in a manner analogous to the way an excise tax on oranges would disturb the natural price ratio of oranges to apples, thus impairing the adaptation of consumption patterns to consumers preference and production potentialities."[7]

The point has been considered in the previous review of Irving Fisher. There is hardly more disturbance of natural exchange ratios between saving and not saving than there is between working and not working. There are no neutral taxes (economically speaking) except poll taxes.

Unlike Fisher, who left the impression that the spendings tax was the last refuge of conservative thought, Vickrey recognized and stressed the potentialities of progression in this area. Although saving increases more rapidly than income as the latter advances, so also may the tax rates on spending. Since the taxpayer has an option and the tax applies presumably to only part of his income, rates above 100 percent may be considered. A gain for equity would occur because people who live high off inheritances or previous accumulation or capital gains would now be forced to render their share. Several

7. William Vickrey, *Agenda for Progressive Taxation* (New York: Ronald Press Co., 1947), p. 336.

proponents of the spendings tax (notably Vickrey and Kaldor) have never conceded that egalitarian objectives cannot be as well (or better) pursued under a spendings tax as under a net income tax.

Vickrey anticipated that a spendings tax (replacing the income tax) would augment savings and also support the incentive to invest and take risks. High graduation, however, might greatly reduce effects of this kind.

Unlike Fisher, Vickrey did not take it for granted that augmented saving would be advantageous. He noted that classical (and other) economics had made little attempt to formulate criteria for the optimum rate of capital formation. Traditionally this had been reduced largely to a comparison of the interest of future generations as against one's own. Pigou and others had thought that one could depend on human nature's propensity to shortchange the future. Vickrey noted that technological and other progress means a consistent secular rise in living standards and that this favors the future over the present. Moreover, Vickrey shared the Keynesian concern that savings may outrun opportunities for investment. But he was not much alarmed that the spendings tax might aggravate an imbalance here; he escaped with the comforting reassurance that, after all, the effects of a flexible spendings tax on total saving need not be very substantial.

Again, the spendings tax might aggravate the concentration of wealth and power. It would open the door for highly acquisitive people to add to their stock indefinitely while paying scarcely any tax. This worried Vickrey. Of course, along with Fisher he looked to the death tax to save the day here. And unlike Fisher, he laid out the blueprints for a much stronger death-tax system. But if this should not prove adequate, Vickrey offered a special antidote, a high-bracket income tax at severe rates on income from equities (stocks) only. The idea apparently was to aim at the power-concentration factor rather than wealth as such.

Vickrey examined administrative prospects for a spendings tax and concluded that they are not promising in the case of the smaller incomes. Too much information concerning capital transactions and status would be required to enforce the tax properly. Accordingly, he expressed his preference for an eclectic package of levies: income tax for small incomes, spendings tax for middle brackets, and anti-power equity income tax at the top.

As we have said, it is Vickrey among tax economists, who has had the keenest appreciation of, and made the greatest contributions toward, the understanding of the *timing* problems in taxation. Unhappily, his proposals involved such flights of the intelligence and imagination that they have had little practical influence. His espousal of the spending tax, which we have here used to give him his classification, was an able and well-balanced treatment. And the *Agenda* as a whole will stand for a long time as a highwater mark in tax inventiveness.

Proponents of a Personal Spendings Tax

Nicholas Kaldor

The British have never seriously entertained the substitution of an expenditure tax for part or all of the income tax. But in many respects a spendings tax would better suit British circumstances than those of the United States. At the time such a tax was proposed in 1955, the outstanding British circumstance was the complete exclusion of capital gains (with minor qualifications) from the income tax base; this supported the charge that the existing system was "absurdly inequitable." British income tax administration is the envy of the world and could carry an extra load perhaps. The British currently could make good use of more capital; at least they are widely convinced that more capital would buttress the industrial improvements needed to hold and enlarge a precarious export market. Under these conditions a proposal to substitute a spendings tax for the income surtax could be very persuasive. Such a proposal came in 1955 from the British economist Nicholas Kaldor.

Nicholas Kaldor is a Fellow of King's College and a Reader of Economics at Cambridge University. He is known as a collaborator with Sir William Beveridge in the work *Full Employment in a Free Society* and has published several articles in economic theory and welfare economics. In 1947–49 he was Director of the Research and Planning Division of the Economic Commission for Europe. He was also a member of the Royal Commission on the Taxation of Profits and Income, 1951–55, from which experience *An Expenditure Tax* was an offshoot.

In a minority report of this Commission, Kaldor and two other commissioners took a vigorous stand for the taxation of capital gains. They struck out against an income tax that makes meticulous effort at adjustments to allow for personal circumstances and yet permits wholesale accruals of economic power to go untaxed. They expressed a doubt that any definition of the term "income" could approximate individuals' spending power as closely as actual spending does. They were foreclosed from pursuing this line of thought by the exclusion of a spendings-tax proposal from the Commission's terms of reference. Accordingly Kaldor wrote his book in self-defense and to supplement the minority report of the Royal Commission.[8]

It was partly due to Kaldor's advice and influence that India enacted an expenditure tax. Although Kaldor's book does not cover underdeveloped economies, it can be said that if countries like India can manage the administrative difficulties of such a measure, it would suit their conditions peculiarly well. Among these conditions are a critical need for capital and the propensity among the rich to indulge in conspicuous consumption.

It will be noted that Kaldor promotes his consumption tax from the left: his point of view is to Irving Fisher's as Galbraith's is to Harley L. Lutz's.

8. Royal Commission on the Taxation of Profits and Income, *Final Report* (London: H.M.S.O., 1955), pp. 354–424.

Fisher gave the impression that he wanted a spendings tax, among other reasons because he preferred leaving capital gains untaxed. Kaldor criticized the income tax because it does not succeed in taxing them.

Kaldor's Personal Spendings Tax

An overall expenditure tax with graduated rates and exemptions is not to be confused with what Kaldor calls a consumption tax in rem—an ordinary sales tax. The latter, he says, is objectionable because it is regressive and makes a crude distribution of the tax load. Moreover, its incidence is uncertain and it can be unneutral as between different patterns of expenditure. None of these sins can be attributed to a personal spendings tax.

As to egalitarian objectives, Kaldor, like Vickrey, holds that an expenditure tax can serve at least as well as an income tax. "A change-over to an expenditure tax would undoubtedly have the most severe effect on the wealthy and not on the people who are only moderately well-off. It would therefore be nonsensical to suggest that an expenditure tax would imply a less progressive method of parcelling out the burden of taxation than the present system."[9] Strong and flexible graduation can be relied upon to do as much equalizing as may be desired. As for the personal needs that dictate spending as against saving for some people, they can be recognized by personal exemptions and other allowances.

It is true, says Kaldor, that the exemption of savings from the income tax might seem like a wide-open invitation to accumulate indefinitely and that with his accumulation might go excessive power. Like others before him, he recommended reliance on the death tax to keep this tendency in bounds. Moreover, power is associated with large-scale industry and firms and cannot be checked very effectively by personal taxation. Preventing acquisition within the life of the taxpayer must inhibit enterprise. "The accumulation of individual fortunes is an inevitable by-product of capitalistic enterprises. It is the entrepreneurial classes, not the rentiers, who are hit by the taxation of savings; the millionaire rentiers, like the landed aristocracy, possess large fortunes but they do not *accumulate* them."[10]

Kaldor's endorsement of the spendings tax is motivated in large part by a concern about the adequacy of saving. Unlike Vickrey he had no concern at all apparently that savings could become redundant. The Keynesian problem of over-saving is a cyclical problem and should not be confused with the issue of long-run growth. Cyclical excesses can be dealt with by budgetary surpluses and deficits. Looking at the secular aspect, he subscribes to the view that savings merely determine the rate of growth in the economy, and growth, no

9. Nicholas Kaldor, *An Expenditure Tax* (London: George Allen and Unwin, 1955), p. 50.
10. Ibid., p. 150.

matter how much or how fast, is all on the side of the angels. "That Britain will require—looking into the distant horizons—a higher rate of growth, to maintain her competitive position in the world, than she has attained in the last fifty-six years is at last becoming generally recognized."[11]

The rich under the income tax do not save much, and indeed it would be irrational for them to try. The income tax is severe in the high brackets, and it discriminates against saving. The argument here is similar to that presented by Vickrey and Fisher (previously discussed).

Economists are agreed, says Kaldor, that the income tax has adverse effect on risk incentives; the option to be or not to be taxed on the gains attending successful risk-taking would surely make the latter more inviting. (But the reviewer wonders how much incentive will be preserved if each increment to saving by the rich (as a class) results in augmented tax rates.) Since people usually spend casual income gradually, the spendings tax would provide a sort of built-in averaging device. If chronic inflation is a problem, as many people have come to believe, the spendings tax would be the ideal weapon for holding the line against this evil. The tax would discourage the spending on consumption goods that feeds inflation; it would not similarly discourage spending on capital goods (investment). Inflationary investment, however, is a trade-cycle problem which can be managed through trade-cycle remedies.

On moral grounds the spendings tax has a strong appeal. It "would tax people according to the amount which they take out of the common pool and not according to what they put into it."[12]

Administration

On the administrative side, it is clear that a spendings tax would require a very competent adminstrative staff and a disciplined tax-paying public. But Britain has both of these essentials. Additional information that would be required is impressive. Mention is made of these items: the purchase and sale of capital assets, money borrowed or lent, bank balances, gifts, capital payments received from life insurance companies, gambling gains and losses. High marginal rates might seem to invite evasion, but evaded tax could not be spent without additional evasion. Moreover, there are not many ways of spending money which are not matters of public information. Nevertheless, it would be wise at the start at least, to replace only the surtax. This need not disturb such well-established institutions as collection at the source and pay-as-you-go withholding.

A rate schedule ranging from 25 to 300 percent is suggested, the latter on expenditure in excess of 5,000 pounds.[13] The suggested rates are less severe than they seem, not only because they do not apply to income saved, but also

11. Ibid., p. 187.
12. Ibid., p. 53.
13. Ibid., p. 241.

because all taxes, excluding only the spendings tax itself, would be deductible from the base. Moreover, the rates as recommended would be mitigated somewhat by the use of the so-called French quotient system, calculating family expenditures for tax purposes at so much per head (total outlay divided by the number within the family). Thus, a family of four could spend 20,000 pounds (some $56,000) without incurring the top-bracket rate. And, if a single person had an income of $1,000,000 and paid $400,000 in income taxes, and if he spent $100,000 of this income on private living he might pay taxes altogether of somewhat less than $700,000. However, if he spent $200,000 the tax would not be far short of confiscatory. Higher rates of spending would have to be financed out of capital.

Conclusion

Kaldor's book performs well the valuable service of calling sharply to attention the unhealthy state of high-bracket income taxation both in Britain and the United States. A tighter law, lower rates, and more stress on a much-improved death tax are the least that are indicated. He performs a service, too, in supplying real flesh and bones to an old idea that warrants serious consideration as a replacement for part or all of the net income tax.

Regarding Kaldor's persuasive book, the reviewer records his reservations as follows:

1. As has been noted, Kaldor promotes the expenditure tax in the name of egalitarianism. But it is not very clear to the reviewer what Kaldor is trying to equalize. It might be possible to manipulate spending tax rates in such manner as to preserve the present distribution of tax burdens by income classes. It might even be possible to achieve more equalization than our imperfect income taxes do. But income could not be equalized at all if everybody consumed equally in absolute amounts. Of course, this will not happen under any tax, but it is what the Kaldor proposal promotes. It is equality of spending and not that of income or fortune which is sought. If the wealthy live like the rest of us, they may otherwise have a free hand. The reviewer is not entirely at ease with this prospect of unleashing the acquisitive economy. Huge fortunes have social and political implications as well as economic ones. And in terms of interpersonal equity what we may have here is a proposal to close all loopholes by opening up one new and enormous one.

2. This might be supported to foster saving. All proponents of a spending tax propound the view that the income tax is unneutral toward savings and they aim to correct this alleged unneutrality. The reviewer's dissent from this view has been presented in an earlier chapter. Assuming that the dissent is sound, we must still reckon with the proposition that the tax system should positively promote saving. There are other means than tax favoritism to promote saving. Any mention of these means—such as the curtailment of advertising

and consumer credit—can be calculated to frighten many who appear to want people to spend freely and yet save a great deal too.

3. The difference between a progressive expenditure tax and a progressive income tax would be for many families largely a matter of timing. These families spend sooner or later what they earn, and over the very long run consumption equals income. Expenditures undoubtedly flow more regularly than income, and the expenditure tax measure thus has the advantage of a built-in averaging feature which would spare the taxpayer some of the penalties which a progressive income tax administers to fluctuating income. On the other hand, the timing would be less felicitous in terms of the taxpayer's immediate circumstances. The times in life when an individual most needs a friend are those in which he has little or no income but must incur considerable expense. These are the times of unemployment, crop failure, the apprenticeship period, a poor business year. Here the canon most at stake is that of convenience. The income tax strikes him *when* he saves, and the spendings tax when he dissaves.

4. The reviewer agrees fully with the author that a spendings tax would be a formidable administrative undertaking. The effect of a 300 percent marginal rate on administration is something about which we have no experience. It would mean that on the doubtful classification of a single dollar of expense, three dollars for taxpayer or government would be at stake. Thus, for instance, the taxpayer might give a dinner for his business friends; if the treat were classified as a business outlay, the expense would be very moderate; but if it were classified as a personal outlay, the cost could run to three times the actual expense of the meal. It is doubtful that so much ought to be staked on the verdict of the administrative process which has many such doubtful questions to decide and for which no infallibility has ever been claimed.

The statement that income could be approximated by observing the scale of the taxpayer's living seems particularly dubious. American administration attempts to do this occasionally in so-called net worth assessments, but the facts so established are usually subject to a wide margin of error and involve great expense for the administration.

We have seen that many nineteenth-century critics of the income tax recognized its theoretical virtues but opposed it on the ground that it was not susceptible to an acceptable score of administration. Studies of income-tax evasion in the United States, such as we have, indicate a loss of revenue of some 8 to 14 percent, distributed very unequally as to sources of income: wages, about 5 percent; farm income, rent and interest, over 50 percent. It is conceded that these data are by no means conclusive and that new innovations in administration may have reduced the leakage in some categories. The data in any event are no grounds for complacency. Some critics have used them to justify an impersonal sales tax, which while it has administrative difficulties of its own, will probably leak at different points and for different people than those involved in income tax evasion. Suffice it for our present purpose to observe that perhaps we had better solve the administrative problems we have before we take on more of them and more difficult ones.

PART IV
Functional and Qualitative Taxation

12

Henry George and Land-Rent Taxation

Typically in the United States and Great Britain taxes are mainly on income and the latter is classified only as to size (for graduation). A dollar from wages and a dollar from rent or profits each counts alike in a universal measure. Property is taxed locally and usually at a uniform rate. Rather than this quantitative approach, one might seek to discriminate among sources and kinds of income and wealth. He might do this on grounds of equity or economy or both. In terms of equity, one can argue that a taxpayer is entitled to the fruits of his own labor but not to the fruits of the labor of others. But most of the school of critics we are about to consider have been especially interested in managing the tax system in such manner that it will conserve and promote the tax base. They thought that the art of taxation, as of economics in general, should aim at augmenting the wealth of nations. They were keenly aware that an undifferentiated tax system penalized the industry and thrift which serve the common good. Perhaps there are ways to get revenue (sources to tax) that would escape these penalties on the economic virtues.

The favorite targets here are inheritance and the rent of land. Someone has said that the national income consists of earnings, findings, and stealings. Proponents of qualitative taxation would classify rent and inheritance in the second category.

For a long time many economists have been impressed with the idea that there is something peculiar about land that should have a bearing on tax policy. Thus, as early as John Locke, the philosophy was abroad that the ultimate incidence of all taxes is on land and that the availability of the opportunity of access to land is a fundamental right.[1] The Physiocrats of eighteenth-century France shared Locke's first idea; they held that only land is productive in an ultimate sense and only it can bear taxes. Even though this meant that landowners must carry the entire load of supporting government, the Physiocrats thought the burden would be lightened because taxes would be discounted by

1. John Locke, *Some Considerations of the Consequences of the Lowering of Interest, and Raising the Value of Money* (London, 1692).

new purchasers who bought land. Here we have formulated and explained the so-called capitalization theory of land-tax incidence. By paying less for property subject to tax, the purchaser would "buy free" of the tax and be in a position to earn on his investment as much as though the tax had not been imposed. A single tax on land would be the simplest and best of all tax systems. The name popularly connected with a single tax on land is that of Henry George. The idea of a special land tax, however, has a rich history that goes back far beyond George.

Land-Rent Taxation and the Classical Economists

Adam Smith failed to follow the Physiocrats in their idea that landlords play an exclusive role in production, but he did concur in the view that ground rent is an especially suitable subject for taxation. Discussing the matter in connection with the house tax, he observed that the portion of the tax which fell on ground rent would not raise rental charges nor discourage industry and that it would reach income enjoyed by its recipient without "any attention of his own."[2]

David Ricardo (1772–1823), who gained a fabulous reputation as a British economist, concerned himself chiefly with the distribution of wealth and income. It was his theory of rent and the role of landlords in society that provided the foundation and inspiration for much subsequent radical thought. We need not undertake to present in detail here Ricardo's celebrated analysis of rent.[3] Ricardo was especially impressed by the relation of rent to the differences in the fertility of land; the rent of the best lands could be conceived as the excess in their productive potential over that of the marginal lands, barely worth cultivating. Add to this conception the Malthusian theory of population, which had recently captured so much attention. With increasing population, and as the margin of cultivation is pushed out to less and less productive resources, high rents follow high prices. Rent contributes nothing to the creation of value but is itself the result of such value. A tax on rent as such could not be shifted (would not disturb prices), but an acreage tax including marginal land would raise the price of corn.

Particularly in the later years of the nineteenth century (overlapping and following Henry George), Ricardian rent theory took a bad beating from the economists. Indeed some historians of economic thought have suggested that nothing is left of it any more except an historical curiosity. Also persuasively attacked was Ricardo's idea that rent does not enter into prices. Herbert Joseph Davenport introduced his re-examination of this old thesis with his famous rhyme, "The Price of Pig":

2. Adam Smith, *Wealth of Nations,* bk. 5, pt. 2, chap. 2, art. 1.
3. David Ricardo, *The Principles of Political Economy and Taxation,* Everyman's Library (New York: E. P. Dutton and Co., 1911), p. 131.

> The price of pig
> Is something big;
> Because its corn, you'll understand,
> Is high-priced too,
> Because it grew
> Upon the high-priced farming land.
>
> If you'll know why
> That land is high,
> Consider this: its price is big
> Because it pays
> Thereon to raise
> The costly corn, the high-priced pig!

Davenport argued that rent is a cost like any other and does raise prices of final products.

Of all the classicists, John Stuart Mill most fully represented and explained the point of view we are here attempting to expound. In a previously quoted passage that will bear repeating, he stated his preference for qualitative selection in taxation as follows:

> To tax the larger incomes at a higher percentage than the smaller is
> to lay a tax on industry and economy; to impose a penalty on peo-
> ple for having worked harder and saved more than their neighbors.
> It is not the fortunes which are earned, but those which are un-
> earned, that it is for the public good to place under limitation.[4]

For one application of this philosophy Mill chose the field of gifts, be-
quests, and inheritances. Not only was this field specially suitable for taxation; it was also suitable for graduation, a technique that Mill was prone to recommend very conservatively. To tax earned wealth would discourage labor; to tax unearned wealth would encourage labor; people could not subsist on the earnings of others and would be obliged to start working.

But the most conspicuous unearned income for Mill was land rent, and as Ricardo had shown, it looked like an ever-increasing claim upon the national income. Ricardo had shrunk from applying the logic of his analysis to tax policy but the more socially minded Mill had fewer inhibitions:

> Suppose there is a kind of income that constantly tends to in-
> crease, without any exertion or sacrifice on the part of the owners:
> those owners constituting a class in the community, whom the
> natural course of things progressively enriches, consistently with
> complete passivity on their own part. In such a case it would be
> no violation of the principles on which private property is founded

---

4. John Stuart Mill, *Principles of Political Economy* (London: Longmans, Green, and Co., 1929), bk. 5, chap. 2, sec. 3, p. 808.

if the state should appropriate this increase in wealth, or part of it,
as it arises. This would not properly be taking anything from anybody; it would merely be applying an accession of wealth, created
by circumstances, to the benefit of society, instead of allowing it
to become an unearned appendage to the riches of a particular
class.[5]

He went on to say that the above fitted the character of rent and of landlords.
Of the existing British land tax which he found to be unfortunately small, he
observed that it should not be regarded as any tax at all but as a rent charge in
favor of the public.

Notwithstanding these brave words, Mill did exhibit considerable reservation about application. He was sensitive to the British tradition of sportsman-
ship, a disinclination to change rules in the middle of a game without due compensation to vested interests. And so he worked out a rather elaborate compromise that would tax only future land increments. It was the American philosopher Henry George who would apply Mill's doctrine without any inhibitions at all.

Henry George

Henry George (1839–1897) is frequently rated by the trade as a journalist
rather than an economist. At any rate, he left school at the age of 14, and if
economist at all, he was one without benefit of a Ph.D. However, he had a
rather complete education in the School of Hard Knocks, having worked at a
great variety of occupations and having been desperately poor. At the age of
15 he went to sea on a vessel bound for Australia and Calcutta and at 19 he
left Philadelphia for California in search of gold. He was unsuccessful in finding the kind of gold he sought and he turned to various jobs, ending as a journalist with the San Francisco newspapers. In California he witnessed the rapid
growth of land values which notched higher with each new load of immigrants.
George's interest in the land question led to the writing of *Progress and Poverty*. George found difficulty in securing a publisher and was obliged to set type
for the first edition himself. But in due time the book achieved a phenomenal
popularity, until today it ranks as one of the best sellers of all time among
economics books.

Soon after publication of his book George migrated to New York. He now
found himself in great demand as a lecturer, at which he proved very effective.
George also became the leader of a movement, and Land and Labor Clubs
were widely organized under his influence. Every movement must have a mar-
tyr; an eloquent Catholic priest, Father McGlynn, who associated himself with
George and his movement was for a time excommunicated.

Because of his interest in the Irish land question George was invited to

5. Ibid., bk. 1, chap. 1.

Henry George and Land-Rent Taxation

Ireland in 1881, and he spent a year in that country and England. He returned to England later for an extensive lecture tour, and much later he also toured Australia and New Zealand, where his welcome was especially impressive and his influence substantial and enduring.

George also took a turn at politics. In 1886 he was a candidate for mayor of New York, running against Theodore Roosevelt and the Tammany candidate Abram S. Hewitt. Hewitt was elected, but George ran second in the poll and succeeded in badly frightening his opposition. In 1897 he was again persuaded to become a candidate for mayor despite failing health, and he died toward the close of the campaign.

George's funeral was an impressive occasion attended by thousands of his friends and followers. The movement which he started continued after him, well-financed by certain endowments and with an ardent but dwindling allegiance. Campaigns were conducted in various states to modify tax laws according to Georgian views, but with little success. Pennsylvania alone has made statutory provisions for a graded-tax plan (improvements assessed at half of full value), and Pittsburgh and Scranton have applied this option for many years.

Progress and Poverty could not be rated as a profound contribution to economics and it made no pretense of judicial treatment. But it was an eloquent book, "written from the heart," and powerfully persuasive.

Henry George's Paradox

George's main problem was that of explaining persistent poverty notwithstanding impressive technical progress. He drew heavily on the classics of Ricardo and Mill, including their view that the landlord takes much from the community and adds nothing. His theory of labor and capital excluded the idea that either exploited the other or the community, each tending to get the benefit of its contribution. This left a single villain in the picture and it was the landlords. They succeed in extracting a large and growing share out of the hides of the other claimants to the national income. Here is the explanation of the paradox that started George on his inquiry.

The landlord's expropriations are peculiarly unjustified because the land is by natural right the heritage of all the people. Private property in land is as inappropriate as private property in men.

A celebrated passage from George at this point will serve to indicate both his philosophy and his style of presentation:

> Take now . . . some hard-headed businessman, who has no
> theories but knows how to make money. Say to him:
> "Here is a little village; in ten years it will be a great city—in
> ten years the railroad will have taken the place of the stage coach,
> the electric light of the candle; it will abound with all the
> machinery and improvements that so enormously multiply

the effective power of labor. Will, in ten years, interest be any higher?"

He will tell you, "NO!"

"Will the wages of common labor be any higher; will it be easier for a man who has nothing but his labor to make an independent living?"

He will tell you, "No; the wages of common labor will not be any higher; on the contrary, all the chances are that they will be lower; it will not be easier for the mere laborer to make an independent living; the chances are that it will be harder."

"What, then, will be higher?"

"Rent; the value of land. Go, get yourself a piece of ground, and hold possession."

And if under such circumstances, you take his advice, you need do nothing more. You may sit down and smoke your pipe; you may lie around like the lazzaroni of Naples or the leperos of Mexico; you may go up in a balloon, or down in a hole in the ground; and without doing one stroke of work, without adding one iota to the wealth of the community, in ten years you will be rich! In the new city you may have a luxurious mansion; but among the public buildings will be an almshouse.[6]

The reviewer will reserve comment on this and George's other views until the end of this chapter. Here he will merely observe that not all American villages have grown (or will grow) into cities and that George's simple formula for making a fortune has been tried by quite a few people with disappointing results.

Along with the explanation of poverty, George set for himself the task of accounting for business crises and depressions. During a considerable part of the post-Civil War era they had been the subject of bitter experience and a matter of wide discussion. George found the answer in land speculation. People insist on holding land which they themselves will not and cannot use, waiting for an eventual rise in price. The crisis or "paroxysm" as George called it, occurs when the normal rent line and the speculative rent line get too far apart. The depression serves to bring the two lines together; idle land is again made available for employment and production. Speculators lose confidence or staying-power and they relinquish their hold on essential resources.

George's Remedy: the Single Tax

As to the remedy for the ills above depicted, George offered a simple prescription: tax away the entire economic rent from land and abolish all other taxes.

In a chapter on "Claims of Landowners to Compensation" George raised

6. Henry George, *Progress and Poverty* (New York: Robert Schalkenbach Foundation, 1931), pp. 293–94.

Henry George and Land-Rent Taxation

the question that had troubled Mill "whether having permitted land to be treated as private property for so long, we should in abolishing it be doing a wrong to those who have been suffered to base their expectations upon its permanence."[7] He considered Mill's compromise solution of taxing only future increments and decided against it. He thought Mill's solution cumbersome in administration. But the overwhelming objection lay in the fact that it "would leave for all the future, one class in possession of the enormous advantage over others which they now have."[8] He noted that originally there had been talk of compensating slave-owners for their loss of property attending emancipation but that emancipation had been consummated without such compensation—and rightly. "If the land belongs to the people, why in the name of morality and justice should the people pay its saleable value for their own?"[9]

The tax on land, because of land's special character, would have a unique and peculiarly favorable incidence. Other taxes must fall on goods or acts that are not of fixed quantity and by the play of economic forces, these taxes would be shifted from seller to buyer, increasing as they go. Land taxes, on the other hand, would decrease the price of land, and the complete recapture of economic rent should reduce it to nothing. Those holding land for use might find that its *market value* had disappeared. But the *usefulness* of the property for them would not disappear; it would serve their purpose as well as ever.

Reviewer's Comments

It is not very difficult, especially with the advantage of some eighty years of history on the reviewer's side, to pick flaws in George's case for a single tax on land. Both he and Marx have fared badly on their notions of increasing misery for the masses. Available evidence indicates that the real income of the general population has risen and that the share of the landlords has been declining.

The practical difficulties in special land taxation were too lightly dismissed by Henry George. Special land taxation is not well adapted to rural property where the distinction between land and improvements cannot be sharply drawn. Particularly where rural and urban property support common services (as in the case of most counties and many school districts) taxing land only could be highly prejudicial to the farmer. In addition, special taxation of land at heavy rates could be expected to have many social effects on cities that have not been adequately studied. The land tax itself is probably neutral as between alternative locations, but substitution of the land tax for the existing property tax is not.

No doubt, the claims made for the single tax were extravagant and justified the attacks on it as a panacea. George had argued that in addition to

7. Ibid., p. 359.
8. Ibid., p. 362.
9. Ibid., p. 364.

supplying the government with ample and costless revenue, his proposal would raise the returns to both labor and capital, abolish poverty, end the business cycle, lessen crime, elevate morals, and "carry civilization to yet nobler heights."

Notwithstanding these and many other valid criticisms of George's doctrine, it contains much that in the reviewer's opinion has stood the test of time. It is true that land (as space and position), unlike capital, is not produced or reproduced and that its value is solely a function of demand. It is true that the supply of land exists independently of man's efforts, investment, and risk-taking. Taxes on it accordingly should be uniquely immune to adverse effects on incentives. There is some truth, too, in the view that a long-standing tax on land is in some sense burdenless on current taxpayers. More important is the fact that land is socially a costless asset; we would still have its services if all rent were appropriated to the government.

Many criticisms of George's doctrine have never seemed convincing to this reviewer. There is, for instance, one that denies the existence of any socially-created increments, contending that all which appear such are produced and paid for in the "ripening cost of land." But on closer analysis these so-called ripening costs are, partly at least, interest and risk on investment that would not exist if the state had expropriated land values. Various writers have regarded increments to land values as an incentive for development in much the same way that percentage depletion in the federal income tax law is regarded as a necessary incentive in the search for oil. However, the market has its own means of compensating risk and effort. It is doubtful that such inducements constitute either an economical or necessary reward to support social objectives.

It has often been, too, that differentials in quality are characteristic of all factors of production and that there is really nothing unique in gifts of nature. But it is also true that the value of land is not dependent upon differentials—scarcity and productivity are enough to account for it. Personal abilities are to some extent a gift of nature, but they are also the result of effort. The existence of other surpluses may be an argument against single taxation of land values, but it is not an argument against any special taxation of such values.

It is fashionable to refer to George's contribution and program today as an historical curiosity, very interesting, but without applicability to the current situation. The reviewer much prefers the verdict that George's contribution contained elements of truth that are of enduring importance. They are currently relevant even if only in support of property taxes as against sales taxes, capital gains' inclusion in the income tax as against their exclusion, and cost as against percentage depletion. There has been a revival of interest in land taxation associated with the problem of urban and metropolitan sprawl. A general urban land tax with money allocated according to origin for general property tax relief deserves much more following than it is likely to attract.

13

Commons, Hobson, and Qualitative Taxation

John R. Commons

Professor Commons (1862–1944) was not a specialist in taxation, and he left no systematic treatment of the subject. The record of his views in this area is largely confined to a relatively short section in his *Institutional Economics.* He is included here because, like the other writers reviewed in this section, he distinguishes between tax treatment of earned income and tax treatment of unearned income—a distinction referred to as "qualitative taxation." Further, he developed ideas about land taxation distinct in some respects from any we have thus far considered.

John R. Commons was born in Indiana where his father, among other pursuits, owned and published a newspaper. Young Commons learned the printing trade which he practiced off and on to earn his way through Oberlin College. He maintained his membership in the typographical union until his death.

As so often happens in college, John R. Commons met with influences there that were destined to shape his entire life. One of these was a course in economic thought taught by a Professor Monroe who had been a Republican congressman and a consul at Rio de Janeiro. It was Monroe also who induced two of the trustees at Oberlin to lend Commons the money for his graduate work at Johns Hopkins University where he met Richard T. Ely, who later was instrumental in his recruitment at the University of Wisconsin. However, Commons failed a history examination at Johns Hopkins, lost his scholarship and never received a Ph.D. degree. Most of the considerable number of degrees he carried in his later years were honorary degrees. (This detail is offered as some consolation for graduate students who have trouble with grades and examinations.)

While at Oberlin, Commons read Henry George's *Progress and Poverty;* he heard George deliver a lecture to Oberlin students; and he became a member of the Georgian Campus Club.

The first half of Commons's life was a succession of failures and discouragements. After his high school graduation he attempted to teach country school; after losing disciplinary control of his pupils, he resigned vowing never to teach again. As we have noted, his graduate career at Johns Hopkins was less than a conspicuous success. On the staff at Wesleyan University, he was notified that he would not be rehired because his lectures failed to interest his students. He remained on the staff at Oberlin for one year only. He stayed longer at Indiana, but when he resigned it was with the impression that the authorities were happy to see him go. His book *Distribution of Wealth* was labeled as disguised socialism and otherwise unfavorably reviewed. At Syracuse, among other things he defended Sunday baseball, incurring the wrath of the religious community, and he was regarded by the chancellor as an impediment in fund raising. He was fired. Employed by George Shibley to develop price index numbers for the Democratic Party, the trend in prices changed perversely and Commons again found himself looking for a new job. On the staff of the Industrial Commission he fared better, but ended his stint with a neuro-intestinal breakdown. His work for the Civic Federation was effective and established for him some reputation as a labor conciliator. On the basis of this and some former association, Richard T. Ely brought him in 1904 to Wisconsin to teach labor-economics courses and finish a project on the history of the labor movement. His fortunes then took a sharp turn for the better. Certainly his association with adversity was long and intimate.[1]

This was the LaFollette era in Wisconsin state politics, and Commons was soon pressed into active duty writing a civil service statute (1905). His contributions to practical governmental (and private) reforms in such areas as labor conciliation, accident compensation, industrial commissions, unemployment insurance, social security, and public utility regulation, along with his monumental *History of Labor in the United States,* his *Legal Foundations of Capitalism,* and his extraordinary success in enlisting the cooperation of his students in research are among the major reasons for his renown.

Commons is classed as an institutional economist, a term extraordinarily difficult to define. Perhaps it is most adequately distinguished as a set of attitudes toward economics and its method, largely shared by the three American economists—Commons, Veblen, and Mitchell. This attitude included, among other things, an interdisciplinary approach to the subject, purposefulness in

---

1. The fullest accounts of John R. Commons' life are found in his autobiography *Myself* (New York: Macmillan Co., 1934; reprinted, Madison: University of Wisconsin Press, 1963) and Lafayette Harter, Jr., *John R. Commons* (Corvallis, Oregon: Oregon State University Press, 1962). For an elaboration of the historical setting and distinctive contributions of the so-called institutional economists, see Joseph Dorfman, "The Background of Institutional Economics," in *Institutional Economics: Veblen, Commons and Mitchell Reconsidered* (Berkeley: University of California Press, 1963), especially the perceptive chapter by Neil Chamberlain on John R. Commons in this symposium.

the direction of effort (Commons's "limiting factor"), emphasis upon empirical research (the latter including first-hand observation of institutions and due respect for their historical development), a distrust of the academic and of deductive theory, advocacy of the free pragmatic use of government to solve human problems, stress on collective action and the conflict of interests, concern about output as contrasted with pecuniary interests, and discernment of the predominantly intangible element in property. The influence of all this on economics and public finance has been profound. Lafayette Harter argues that it has now so engulfed the general stream of economic thinking that it no longer needs advocacy or a self-conscious following. To this general conclusion the reviewer has elsewhere taken exception.[2] So pronounced were Commons's views against much of the academic product of his day that he might be labeled by certain critics as anti-intellectual.

Commons on Taxation

Commons started his analysis of taxation with the proposition that all taxes have important non-fiscal effects if not a non-fiscal purpose. The section of his *Institutional Economics* devoted to taxation bears the significant title "The Police Power of Taxation." His point of view on this matter is forcefully stated as follows:

> Taxation, then, is the most pervasive and privileged exercise of the police power . . . Even when not consciously intended to be regulative, taxes nevertheless regulate, for they, like the protective tariff, determine the directions in which people may become wealthy by determining the directions in which they may not become wealthy. They say to the businessman: Here is profit, there is loss. It is impossible to escape the police power of taxation, therefore impossible to look upon taxes of any kind whatever as merely means of obtaining revenue according to any principle of equality, or ability to pay, or accumulation of wealth or any standard that looks solely to the acquisitions of the past. Taxation is, in fact, a process of obtaining revenue by proportioning inducements to obtain profit.[3]

Commons's main interest and objective in taxation can be perceived in what he called his canon of taxation, which he stated as follows:

> But if there is another canon of taxation that may be properly applied, namely, the effects on wealth production guided by the public purpose of favoring wealth production, then the man who

2. Harold M. Groves, "Institutional Economics and Public Finance," *Land Economics* 40 (August 1964).
3. John R. Commons, *Institutional Economics* (New York: Macmillan Co., 1934), p. 20.

gets his wealth by a mere rise in site values should pay proportionately higher taxes than the one who gets his wealth by industry or agriculture. In the one case, he extracts wealth from the commonwealth without adding to it. In the other case, he contributes directly to an increase in both private wealth and commonwealth. Hence, looking at it from the commonwealth, or social utility standpoint, there are two kinds of ability to pay: that ability which varies directly with one's addition to the commonwealth, and that which varies inversely to one's additions to the commonwealth. The first we shall name the Ability to Serve, the second, Ability to Pay, . . . Taxes should be apportioned directly according to ability to pay and inversely according to ability to serve.[4]

This is good individualist and capitalist philosophy: it is no crime to get rich as long as you do so by raising the general level; it is different when you get rich at the expense of your neighbors. Commons shows how the early courts of England sought to establish rules of economic conduct on a similar philosophy. The clearest cases of getting wealth from others are those of fraud and theft, and these shade into more subtle devices. Unfortunately, notes the reviewer, the lines between wealth and commonwealth, never too clear, become sadly blurred in an era of oligopoly. Commons's ideas were similar to those expressed by Mill, but some of the inspiration probably came from John Locke, whom Commons studied assiduously.

In the application of this theory of proper taxation, Commons recommended several possibilities for reaching surpluses in economic rent. He spoke a good word for special assessments, already in considerable use. Such levies are generally confined to land and are an attempt to recapture the increments resulting from public improvements. In addition, a classified income tax, applying differential rates to favor earned income as Commons defined that term, was suggested. A graduated tax on site values was proposed, including unique features designed to separate and exclude such intangible improvements as soil fertility. Finally, he gave his approval to the classified assessment system of Pittsburgh, under which, in the application of the property tax, land values are more heavily weighted than improvement values.

Professor Commons prepared the Grimstad Bill for submission to the Wisconsin legislature. The bill embodied a proposal for a state tax on bare land values. In his remarks before legislative committees while the Grimstad Bill was pending, Professor Commons gave an elaboration of his views.[5] Starting with the contention of manufacturers that they were over-burdened with taxation, he cited what he considered greater burdens on public utilities and farmers. Nevertheless, he thought that the manufacturers had a point in contending

4. Ibid., p. 819.
5. Remarks by Professor J. R. Commons at a Committee hearing on Bill 532 A, mimeographed (Madison: Legislative Reference Library, March 15, 1923).

against more taxes on industry. The state should avoid tax policies leading to suppression. Why not tax monopoly values and unearned income? He cited the case of the Plankington Arcade in Milwaukee covering less than two acres, with land value of $4 million and improvement value of $3 million, the former about equal to land values in a good Wisconsin township, where however they were divided among hundreds of farmers and half the land value consisted of fertility maintained by "blood and sweat."

Reviewer's Comments

The underlying proposal of the Grimstad Bill is mildness and humility itself compared with the single tax. All it says is that gifts of nature with their scarcity values that the owner did not create are an especially strategic factor to tax. It bears the marks of a compromise—in this case a compromise between the author's interest in equality, served by progressive taxation, and his interest in economy and efficiency, served by qualitative discrimination. However, it will occur to the critic that land values may be a species of a larger genus. Why not tax (specially) all unearned income or wealth? And this question leads us straight into the work of John A. Hobson.

John A. Hobson

John A. Hobson (1857–1940) was an English economist, who was educated in the classics at Oxford but attained no distinguished academic post. To a lesser degree than Henry George, he belongs to the underworld of economics. For a time he was employed by the London University Extension Lectures, but his attack on thrift in his *Of the Physiology of Industry* (1889) ran so against the conventional wisdom of the English heritage that he lost his job. The incident is a potent reminder that in the prevailing British philosophy the practice of thrift ranked in sanctity close to religion. In Hobson's book (co-authored with Memmery) he developed an underconsumption theory of the business cycle and unemployment. For Hobson, unequal bargaining power begets maldistribution; this causes oversaving and underconsumption; and these in turn beget industrial crises and (as developed in a later book) lead to imperialism. It is generally recognized and fully acknowledged that Keynes drew heavily on this heresy and, with modifications, made it quasi-respectable at least for a time. He paid tribute to Hobson's book as follows: "Though it is so completely forgotten today, the publication of this book marks, in a sense, an epoch in economic thought."[6]

Hobson had no rigorous training in economic theory, and he spent much of his life as a free lance writer, mostly for the popular reader. His copious product included fifty-three books in forty-nine years, besides scores of

---

6. John Maynard Keynes, *The General Theory of Employment Interest and Money* (New York: Harcourt, Brace and Co., 1936), p. 365.

periodical articles. He wrote too much and too fast to do it all well but he surely was not short of original ideas, and some of his work, such as his *Evolution of Modern Capitalism* (1894, with several revised editions and reprintings), involved solid scholarship. His views on taxation appeared largely in a single volume entitled *Taxation in the New State,* which was published in 1920. He was a devoted student of John Ruskin and his approach was that of a humanist economist.[7]

Hobson's main original contribution in the field of taxation literature was his idea of economic surplus and its application to tax problems. To be sure, the idea of surpluses of one sort or another was not new in the economic literature. The old French socialists had denounced certain sources of income, particularly rent and inheritance, as special privilege and this philosophy had been accepted for the most part by John Stuart Mill. Many others, including Henry George, Leon Walrus, and John Commons, had singled out the rent of land as *unearned* income in the economic sense of that term. Going further, Karl Marx had added interest and profit to the special-privilege list. Keynes too was to question the reward for saving (interest), which latter he regarded as effortless and void of sacrifice. Both Keynes and Gesell before him questioned the social necessity of interest, regarding it as a purely monetary phenomenon quite divorced from the supply of savings and physical capital. Walker had extended the idea of rent to explain profits, and many economists have noted that an element similar to rent may occur in other factors than land.

Surplus for Hobson was the excess over what is "physically and morally necessary to secure continued use of the factor of production whose owner receives it."[8] He agreed with the economists who had been arguing that rent or something similar to rent—call it surplus—is an ubiquitous phenomenon, and he proposed to build his tax system around the idea of capturing it wherever it occurs. As to the latter, however, he had his own distinctive ideas. Examining the factors of production, one by one, he first conceded the long-standing idea that the rent of land is a genuine surplus. But in our modern society it is only one of many such surpluses and should neither be overemphasized nor singled out for special treatment. Income from monopoly in land is not economically different from other kinds of monopoly incomes that are due to manipulated scarcities and differences in bargaining strength. There are elements of surplus in all rewards of all factors of production, and it would be discriminatory and unwise to single out one of them for taxation. An exception lies in standard wages in any trade or location; they are a necessary cost

7. For a recent work on Hobson's life and writings, see E. E. Nemmers, *Hobson and Underconsumption* (Amsterdam: North-Holland Publishing Co.; New York: Kelley and Millman, 1956).

8. J. A. Hobson, *Taxation in the New State* (New York: Harcourt, Brace and Howe, 1920), p. 14.

of production in that if they are not paid, the requisite supply of labor will not be forthcoming.

There is also a minimum wage for capital, a necessary rate of interest, adequate to induce the saving classes to withhold enough spending power to supply necessary capital. The same analysis can be applied to profits, but Hobson was particularly impressed by what he regarded as a very large element of surplus in this area, this being due to the prevalence of monopoly and the failure of competition to do an adequate policing job. Some reinvestment for a reasonable rate of growth was accepted as a necessary cost or in any event a productive surplus.

On the above foundation Hobson developed a theory of taxation that included considerations of equity, economy, incidence, and incentive, none of them in conflict. As to equity, there is no real ability to pay where there is no surplus, and we couldn't tax it if there were. As to economy, there is obvious advantage in placing taxes where they cannot interfere with output. As to incidence, only a surplus (by definition) can bear a tax. Costs are associated with things that have an elastic supply; that is, these things will tend to disappear if taxed and in doing so, raise prices. This is standard incidence theory. Rising prices will pass the tax on to a surplus and in doing so recoup the economic necessities of producers remaining in the field. It is a painful process and one that it is unwise to inaugurate. As to incentives, these too are covered in Hobson's definition of surplus. When a necessary incentive is attacked at any point, supply will be diminished.

Hobson's Surplus and the Tax System

Although Hobson's analysis might seem to indicate an easy road to a simple and scientific tax system, it suffers greatly from the inability to divide surplus from costs with any degree of precision. Hobson in the end would settle for a steeply graduated general income tax (with adequate exemptions) and of course the death tax, as most likely to achieve his goal of reaching surplus and avoiding costs. His income tax would make no important differentiation of income by sources. In Hobson's own phrasing, "The practical basis of sound taxation is found in the presumption that the proportionate taxable capacity of individual incomes varies directly with their size, i.e., the larger the income, the larger the proportion of taxable surplus it contains."[9]

The death tax would be highly serviceable both to keep the income tax within reasonable bounds and to catch surplus wealth missed by the income tax. The two levies are complementary in character. The local property tax did not appeal to him, but he conceded that a local tax on land values within prescribed limits might be appropriate for local government. This was his one concession to the Georgian point of view. However, he concluded that the

9. Ibid., p. 234.

Functional and Qualitative Taxation

rental value of occupied houses might be the best available index of surplus at the local level. It should be applied with personal exemptions and graduation.

Thus Hobson bridged the gap between qualitative and quantitative taxation and came out with the same answer on either approach. However, he reached and supported his conclusion on grounds quite distinct from those of the equity school.

Reviewer's Conclusion

As previously stated, Hobson's dichotomy of costs and surpluses is logically satisfying but not very helpful practically. What it amounts to mostly is drawing an answer by restating a problem. The problem is to differentiate qualitatively, and Hobson ends by differentiating quantitatively. It looks like a failure to achieve an end, but Hobson can be forgiven perhaps on the score that much differentiation is not possible. The problem is more difficult now than it was one hundred years ago, when it could be argued that all business income is *earned* because earned income is best defined as competitive income and competition is all but universal.

Although Hobson avoids the reliance upon psychological imponderables that plague marginal utility analysis, he plunges us back into a different area of psychology when he stakes his whole structure on incentives about which, until recently at least, we have had virtually no empirical information. And recent empirical studies of incentives have left the impression that they are much less sensitive to high taxes than had been supposed.

Hobson's surplus analysis is vulnerable on other grounds. His concession to the needs of economic growth gives away much of his flimsy case. What might be surplus for the individual or single business might not be surplus for the system as a whole. The confusion just noted can also be applied to Hobson's notion that there is no surplus in basic union wages. Probably one firm could not get a supply of labor were it to offer less than enough to provide the conventional necessities, but if wages were universally taxed to preclude these goods they would cease to be conventional.

After pondering these subtleties in John Hobson's conception one is prone to return to John Commons's idea of specially taxing the clear and pure case of surplus in the economic rent of land, relying on progressive taxation not so much to reach other (indistinguishable) surpluses as to serve egalitarian ends.

Qualitative considerations and economic effects of taxes are always entitled to attention and respect. For instance, one may note in passing that some substitution of an effective death tax for upper-bracket income taxes makes sense in terms of economic effects, that tax-exempt securities on this as well as other counts are ill advised, that at the local level, land taxes make a better choice than personal property taxes or sales taxes. But the difficulties of definition and separation circumscribe severely the role which qualitative considerations can play in ordering a modern tax system.

Commons, Hobson, and Qualitative Taxation

This concludes the treatment of the four main lines of tax philosophy we have sought to trace. One aspect of taxation that weaves in and out of all four schools is its role in fiscal policy. Current treatment of this aspect owes much to renewed interest in aggregative economics. A powerful influence in the renewal has been John Maynard Keynes. To him we now turn.

14

Keynes and Taxation for Aggregative Goals

During most of our budgetary history, according to Louis Kimmel,[1] the federal budget was subject to four constraints:

1. A budget should never be in deficit by design; deficits may on occasion
prove inevitable but financial stability and confidence require a constant effort
to prevent this.
2. Public debt should be avoided and when incurred should be retired as
promptly as possible.
3. The rules of prudence in the private household apply also to the economy as a whole. (Later critics were to illustrate the likely fallacy here with a
simple illustration: if one man brings a stool to the county fair and perches
himself on it in order to view the horse races, the maneuver will be successful;
if everybody were to do this, at best, nobody would profit.)
4. Minimal government (with few qualifications) is beneficial to the private economy and in accord with the public interest.[2]

To these perhaps should be added a fifth precept: Taxation is nature's
sanction for public expenditure, and to divorce the two is an open invitation
to corruption. It would be a case of seeking something for nothing.

Anyone at all familiar with predominant current attitudes towards budgets and the public debt must concede that, for better or for worse, some sort
of revolution has occurred. To most current critics, expenditures without

1. See Louis H. Kimmel, *Federal Budget and Fiscal Policy, 1789–1958* (Washington,
D.C.: Brookings Institution, 1959).
2. While this was the prevailing doctrine, it should be noted that it was never strictly followed in practice. Indeed, it can be argued with plausibility that from the earliest
days of the Republic the unrecognized doctrine that government is the partner of business
and must exercise a positive and beneficent role in this capacity was applied. Business seldom failed to demand from the government any action that would redound to its advantage. On this view it is more the conditions of the economy that have changed rather
than practiced doctrine. But however the change be defined, it must be recognized that it
is both wide and real.

Keynes and Taxation for Aggregative Goals

taxation are not sinful if they will relieve slack in the private economy. Forsaking the Puritan ethic, men have rallied behind the slogan that the budget is
an economic and not a moral document.

To make matters worse for the surviving Puritans, proponents couched this
new heresy in a bewildering array of paradoxes, each an affront to common
sense: the way to save more is to save less; the way to balance the budget is to
unbalance it further; the way to reduce the public debt is to incur more of it;
the way to get more revenue is to reduce taxes; the way for businessmen to
make more profits is to aim at less—cutting prices for instance. Of course, it
must be conceded that the New Testament offers at least one paradox and a
big one: "For whoever would save his life will lose it." But the convinced Puritan could see the hand of that old deluder Satan in all this fancy economics.

We have observed that many public finance economists repeated the canons
of Adam Smith and added one of their own which they labeled *adequacy*. But
the concept was confined to the yield of specific taxes or the capacity of the
tax system to meet the recognized needs of government. No new content appeared in this old bottle; adequacy became a matter of taxes being high enough
to prevent inflation in the private economy.

Although the revolution in attitudes recounted above was partly the result of experience prior to John Maynard Keynes, his famous book, *The General Theory of Employment, Interest and Money* (1936), gave the outlook systematic articulation and was vastly influential in confirming the trend.

John Maynard Keynes (1883–1946) was a British economist of fabulous
influence, reputation, and brilliance. His father, Neville Keynes, was a Cambridge economist of some reputation and his mother was an able woman, at
one time mayor of Cambridge. The younger Keynes was by all testimony mag-
nificently endowed, and everything he touched turned to success. He was educated at Eton and Cambridge, where he was highly successful in his studies, in
debate, and even to some extent in athletics. He acquired a proficiency in
mathematics, and one of his early books was on probability. But at Cambridge,
where he encountered Alfred Marshall and A. C. Pigou, he showed an early preference for economics. After graduation he worked for a time in the India office
but later returned to Cambridge as lecturer on economics and politics. From
1912 to 1944 he was editor of the *Economic Journal*. During World War I, he
was employed by the British Treasury and assigned to work on overseas finances.
In 1919 he represented the Treasury at the Paris Peace Conference; on the basis
of this experience he wrote *The Economic Consequences of the Peace* (1919),
which established his reputation. The book was highly critical not only of the
peace itself but of its celebrated individual architects.

In 1925 he was married to Lydia Lopokova, a popular and beautiful
dancer. The marriage, like almost everything else that Keynes undertook, was
a complete success. Keynes is said to have observed that his temperamental
wife was even less predictable than the economy. But he seems to have managed very well in both areas.

Keynes wrote a half dozen notable books, of which we may confine our attention to the two most influential in public finance: *How to Pay for the War* (1940) and the *General Theory,* previously mentioned. The book on war finance applied Keynesian economics to the inflationary period and introduced the idea of compulsory saving.

In 1937, at fifty-four years of age, Keynes suffered a heart attack and was plagued with this illness for the remaining nine years of his life. Nevertheless, he served his country during World War II in several important diplomatic roles, and he is credited with the principal authorship of the International Monetary Fund inaugurated at Breton Woods.

Keynes lived no cloistered life, and the multiplicity of his interests and achievements outside of economics are as fabulous as his books. He gave thirteen years of his short life to the government and proved a highly competent administrator and diplomat; he dabbled in investments as a hobby and amassed a fortune of well over $2 million; he was president of an insurance company and a Director of the Bank of England; he was a promoter and collector of the arts.

Despite a reputation for radicalism and his frank assessment of the capitalistic system (between the World Wars) as a failure, he was no socialist nor had he any love for bureaucracy. His political association was with the Liberal not the Labor Party.

In the annals of economics there are many types of top-ranking scholars— some that have tasted failure and privation and some that have capitalized on endowment and opportunity with success from the beginning. Keynes was of the latter type—a sort of combination of Mill and Ricardo, more original than the former, more gifted as a writer than the latter. Like many of the great economists he hit the jackpot with a document that rode the dominant interest of his time.

Saving

Selecting a few aspects of Keynesian and post-Keynesian economic thought that suit our present context, we may begin with the argument concerning the nature of saving, the probable adequacy or inadequacy of aggregate saving, and the bearing of these on unemployment. The latter was said to be due principally to maladjustment between intended savings and intended investment. Intended savings are largely a function of income rather than the rate of interest; the higher the rate of income, the more will be saved. This approach may be termed a residual theory of saving; it is supported by common sense, Engel's law of personal expenditures, and the marginal utility concept of the diminishing importance of consumption goods as more are acquired. In the Keynesian view, saving entails no sacrifice and interest could be abolished—except that it is required in a capitalistic economy to ensure parting with liquidity. In an affluent economy, saving tends to become redundant; individual saving is hardly needed at all; business depreciation reserves plus institutional saving would prove adequate. Even in less affluent periods of history, redundant saving was a mischief-maker; it has been a chronic problem of capitalism since the latter's earlier days. Keynes had no faith in the view that business can absorb any amount of savings, the amount simply determining the rate of economic growth. The businessman must have a visible market before he will make a decision to invest. This is not to say that the rate of profit is of no importance; on the contrary, it is the expected rate of profit on new investment that in some sense determines the level of investment.

Although this heresy was not entirely new by any means, it struck a hard, fresh blow at the conventional wisdom. Mandeville's poetry had been banned and Hobson had been fired from his job for saying less. The classical economists, notably Pigou, had almost unanimously stressed the critical importance of saving; they regarded it as the means by which men add to their productivity by equipping themselves with tools. They saw men's natural tendency to pursue the pleasures of the moment at the expense of the future as the principal limiting factor in economic progress. Moreover, the Keynesian view offended the so-called Puritan ethic—that the way to salvation in this world and the next is self-denial. As to redundancy, the classicist's view was that expressed by Carver, who conceded that a community might conceivably save too much but that such a possibility was so rare as to be unknown.[3]

Keynes offered no empirical verification of his doctrine and post-Keynesian criticism of it has been vehement and voluminous. It is fair to say that economists are still in search of an adequate theory of the propensity to save and consume. But much of the Keynesian doctrine in this area has proved highly vulnerable.

Simon Kuznets and others who have studied the volume of saving in a historical-statistical context have found no upward trend in the propensity to save over the decades as the American economy gained in terms of national income and per-capita income. On the contrary, Kuznets notes a considerable drop in relative net capital formation from 1870 to the present, and while this might be either cause or effect of less saving, he inclined toward the latter explanation. Of course, saving itself is not easily measured; accepted methods, for instance, take no account of intangible elements such as outlay for education. Kuznets's figures distinguish sharply between net and gross capital formation; it is the former which has dropped, indicating an increase in depreciation and obsolescence, probably due to the relative rise in machinery capital and the augmented pace of technological progress.[4]

Duesenberry introduced what might be termed a relativity theory of

3. Joseph Dorfman, *The Economic Mind in American Civilization* (New York: Viking Press, 1949), 3: 355.
4. Simon Kuznets, "Proportion of Capital Formation to National Product," *American Economic Review, Papers and Proceedings* 42 (May 1952): 507-26.

consumption and saving which describes any one person's propensities in terms of how his neighbors behave. It may well be that many poor people live better in most respects than Henry VIII; the reason for their discontent is that their neighbors also live better. Along with the technological improvement of consumers goods and the arts of selling them, this could very well account for the fact that a rising gross national produce over time need not mean that people will spend less and save more relative to their incomes.[5]

Friedman argues that the statistics which show that relatively the rich save more than the poor are misleading because annual data include those who are temporarily above and below their normal status. If this fallacy were eliminated, the data would show, he believes, that there is little, if any, relation between the level of income and the propensity to consume. Propensities do differ and this is accounted for by differences in wealth (relative to income) and by certain institutional factors.[6]

The issue of who saves how much is also relevant in appraising sales taxes. If people of all levels of income spend about the same proportion of their incomes upon consumption goods, the alleged regressivity of the sales tax would disappear and indeed it has been so alleged.[7] However, it is not only saving that escapes the typical retail sales tax but also taxes and many services.[8] And this analysis assumes perfect forward shifting of the tax.

Bronfenbrenner has attacked the Kenyesian historical generalization with one of his own, namely that secular inflation has been the general rule throughout recorded history. The nineteenth century was one of the more stable ones in this respect; it also produced a fine record of growth and its depressions did cure themselves in time without (much) governmental intervention. What with the Full Employment Act, labor union pressures, cold war, augmenting population, and so forth, the future looks more inflationary than ever.[9]

Progressive Taxation

Keynes's comments on taxation embrace only a few pages,[10] but they were packed with meat for the proponents of progressive taxation. He observed

5. James S. Duesenberry, *Income, Saving and the Theory of Consumer Behavior* (Cambridge: Harvard University Press, 1952).

6. Milton Friedman. *A Theory of the Consumption Function* (Princeton: Princeton University Press, for the National Bureau of Economic Research, 1957).

7. See David G. Davies, "Progressivity of Sales Taxation in Relation to Various Income Bases," *American Economic Review* 50, no. 5 (December 1960): 987–95.

8. For discussion, see Daniel C. Morgan, Jr., *Retail Sales Tax, An Appraisal of New Issues* (Madison: University of Wisconsin Press, 1964).

9. Martin Bronfenbrenner, "Some Neglected Implications of Secular Inflation," in *Post-Keynesian Economics,* ed. Kenneth Kurihara (New Brunswick: Rutgers Universith Press, 1954), chap. 2.

10. John Maynard Keynes, *The General Theory of Employment, Interest and Money* (New York: Harcourt, Brace and Co., 1936), pp. 372–74.

that since the end of the nineteenth century considerable progress had been made in the use of taxation to reduce disparities in the distribution of wealth and income, especially in Great Britain. But always there was a big inhibition —the fear that such taxation would encroach on the capital needed for growth. Keynes disposed of this impediment with the observation that growth is dependent on abundant saving only under conditions of full employment; otherwise, more saving only impedes growth along with other undesirable consequences.

Hitherto Adam Smith's first and last canons—dealing with equity and economy—had been thought to be in conflict that dictated a compromise solution. Keynes resolved the conflict, and to many proponents of progressive taxation this message seemed like an emancipation proclamation.

True, Keynes noted that the incentive for risk-taking still needed preservation, but he was of the opinion apparently that this could be done within the context of a severely progressive tax system.

Of course, this Keynesian support for progressive taxation is dependent in some degree upon the validity of his conclusion concerning the relationship of the propensity to save with levels of income. Several studies have followed that purported to show that the effect on saving of shifting our tax system from a progressive to a regressive pattern would be rather minor.[11] They argue that the *marginal* propensities to consume are less sensitive to such change than differences in average propensities by income classes would lead one to expect. The hypothesis is offered that this is due, in considerable part, to the fact that the recipients of very small incomes are frequently dissaving and a dissaver's marginal propensity to consume is very low. Instead of enlarging his consumption when his income improves, what he does is to dissave less. These findings are also compatible with the relativity theory of spending; progressive taxation compresses the distribution of income by classes of income, and an improvement of status or the reverse for income recipients by class of income size might not greatly affect the total savings-consumption ratio.

But in one respect, these findings are a support for progressive taxation. If the amount of savings are not greatly affected by tax-induced changes in the distribution of income, gone is the fear that such taxation will undermine the adequacy of savings.

Built-in Flexibility

A further point for progressive taxation with Keynesian associations is built-in flexibility. In the case of almost all taxes, the volume of revenue will fluctuate not only in response to a change in tax rates but also in response to

11. For instance, see Harold Lubell, "Effect of Income Redistribution on Consumer Expenditures," *American Economic Review* 38 (March 1947): 157; see also Richard A. Musgrave, *Theory of Public Finance* (New York: McGraw-Hill Book Co., 1959), pp. 268–71.

Functional and Qualitative Taxation

a change in income. This is particularly true of a progressive tax system where automatic fluctuations in revenue will be greater than the fluctuations in income. In the case of the individual income tax, more income per taxpayer means heavier effective rates even though nominal rates do not change. When Jones's income rises from $2,000 to $4,000, his income tax might quadruple. In the case of the corporate income tax, the fluctuations in revenue greater than those in national income are due to the tendency of corporate profits to fluctuate more than other elements of income. Built-in flexibility is a function of large budgets as well as progressive ones; here high taxes play a beneficial role and the achievement of full-fledged peace (with its accompanying decrease in the size of the federal budget) might aggravate economic instability. It has been calculated that under conditions in the middle 1950's the built-in flexibility factor in public finance in the United States might compensate for fluctuations in private incomes to the extent of some 40 percent of their magnitude.[12]

No doubt the greatest and least controversial of the contributions of aggregative economics to tax philosophy and practice was the new attention it gave to the level of taxation. As has been said, adequacy became a matter of the effects of taxes on the balance in the private economy. Pressed to its ultimate degree, this says that budgets should be balanced only in times of full employment. This doctrine in large degree is now accepted in Great Britain on a non-partisan basis. The massive support for the Revenue Act of 1964 indicates that the new philosophy has penetrated wide and deep in the United States as well.

Of course, there are other alternatives: monetary policy in lieu of fiscal policy, deficits (surpluses) by expenditure manipulation, institutional changes which would affect chronic unemployment directly. But at least while tax cutting is the prescription, tax manipulation appears to lead in popularity. The Keynesians would use monetary policy in a supplementary role, but they have little confidence in its efficacy, particularly in deep depression when reducing interest rates may fail to induce people to part with liquidity.

Now that Keynes has helped to focus attention on the role of taxation in aggregative or macro economics, one is led to recall other tax proposals in this context. One of the oldest and most discussed proposals for combating deep depression is stamped money (i.e., a tax on idle money). This, as Gesell indicated, would make currency depreciate like other goods that serve as a storehouse of value. Among other things, the idea raises some definitional questions in monetary economics. In this day, surely an idle bank balance has to be classed as idle money. Suppose the depositor shifts his account to a time deposit. If the money still remains idle, is this now the bank's hoarding? Would it help much to force money out of idleness and into riskless securities, creating competition which would raise the prices of these securities?

12. Musgrave, *Theory of Public Finance*, p. 511.

Keynes and Taxation for Aggregative Goals

Turning to another persuasive proposal, we note that very large sums are spent annually for advertising. Presumably advertising plays a considerable and perhaps beneficent role in sharpening the propensity to spend. But couldn't this stimulus be turned on and off a bit in the interest of stabilization? This could take the form either of curbs on the deductibility of advertising expense or a direct tax on advertising when strategic.[13] From the social angle there is much to be said for a tax on advertising (see Henry Simons) apart from its potential as a stabilizer. Much of it, like armaments, is a competitive cost which cancels out when all competitors make use of it. But we need not tarry long on the economic difficulties of this proposal. The vested interests involved are so powerful as to relegate the issue to that class of subjects which may be academically attractive but which are politically impossible.

Perhaps the most attractice of the control devices that use taxation in some degree is the Swedish experiment, with corporate reserves stimulated by tax forbearance and ultimately favored through depreciation allowances if they are invested according to government order as to timing. The idea merits further attention in the United States.

13. See Max A. Geller, *Advertising at the Crossroads* (New York: Ronald Press, 1952).

15

Conclusion

We shall not attempt to summarize the many views on taxation presented in this book. Nor shall we attempt to expound a comprehensive view of our own. This chapter presents a few of the reviewer's reflections on what we have covered and their bearing on specific tax issues.

Rationalism in Taxation

On questions of tax policy the reviewer generally finds himself in the ranks of what we have called the rationalists. They are the group which holds that taxes must make sense in terms of distribution. If A pays more than B, we should be able to tell him why. And a defensible answer must be in terms of some factor relevant to his governmental responsibilities. Taxation differs from robbery in several respects, but the most important respect is a rational as against a capricious pattern of distribution. It may not be possible to maintain a rational tax system in an irrational world. But a rational critic need not approve of irrational conduct.

We cannot claim that distribution is the only matter to consider. Taxes, like other public-policy questions, have to be judged by *all* of their consequences. If it can be shown for instance, that of two taxes, one divides a small pie fairly, while the other makes for a much bigger pie less equitably apportioned, we may decide for the second levy. But the rationalist is likely to resolve a doubt in favor of equitable distribution.

Take the opportunist's preference for special excises on the score that they provide the taxpayer an option and that they minimize taxpayers' resistance, do little harm to incentives, and encourage savings. The rationalist first notes that if the option is exercised, the taxpayer avoids governmental responsibilities that are probably his duty. And if it be conceded that some of the collateral effects are favorable, he notes that they must be weighed against the fact that these taxes can interfere with the optimum allocation of resources, curtailing welfare without filling the treasury.

For the rationalist, the principal objection to the retail sales tax is not its regressivity but its crudeness. It mixes a consumption tax which covers only part of consumption with a haphazard business tax of uncertain incidence, and hopes for an impartial outcome.

Income taxes, too, are not free of irrational features and their irrationality is undoubtedly much enhanced by uneven administration. Their principal merit here is that the irrationalities are less inherent in the system and more amenable to reform than is the case with their alternatives.

High on the list of income tax irrationalities is the corporate levy with its uncertain incidence. A persuasive case can be made for replacing much of this feature with a value-added tax, some levy on undistributed earnings, and the full taxation of personal capital gains. But the value-added tax itself might prove easy prey for political favoritism and its incidence again would be none too certain. Since what we seek is a broad-based tax, would it not be better to consider a direct levy on adjusted gross (net) personal income which, like the value-added tax, would aim at the entire national income? The latter levy would afford the opportunity for some minimal family exemption as a concession to the view that it makes no sense to begin a war on poverty with a levy that renders minimum amenities less accessible to the poor.

Whether our elaborate system of personal exemptions and deductions have on balance added to the rationality of the tax system is arguable. Certainly one's family responsibilities are not irrelevant in determining who are the equals to be treated equally. Nor are they irrelevant in weighing the social costs of tax levies. On the other hand, it is surely possible to refine an income tax to death. A system which defined equals in terms of total family income and distributed taxes accordingly and with punctilious care would probably rate better in terms of horizontal equity than does our present more ambitious system as it works in practice.

The persuasive case for opportunism in taxation is that of J. Kenneth Galbraith, who seems to be saying in substance that the end of better nourished public services justifies most any means of raising the money that can gain political acceptance. As we have said, one such means that is rising in popularity is the public lottery. We have found this case unconvincing, at least when better means to the same end are available. Good ends may at times justify bad means, but the means are important and have a way of adversely affecting the ends they serve.

Egalitarianism and Progressive Taxation

The reviewer regards himself as an egalitarian economist. We have been at pains to point out that there is a sharp difference between an egalitarian and a socialist. The former can support a pluralistic society and the latter can support institutions that generate inequalities as wide, perhaps, as those of unmitigated capitalism. We need hardly say that both egalitarianism and socialism can be matters of degree.

Egalitarianism may be espoused as a pure value judgment on the score that the ethic of distribution associated with the private family is preferred to that which comes out of the market place. This was the egalitarianism of Henry Simons.

But egalitarianism may also be supported in terms of its by-products. One of these, in the reviewer's view, is a viable and stable democracy. Egalitarianism within limits is both a means and a goal in a democratic society and government. It helps to keep conflict within bounds and to prevent the extreme polarization of opinion. Income and wealth are political power and the distribution of wealth follows the distribution of income. Any minority, perhaps any majority, that is too poor to have access to the vehicles of communication is prone to the politics of frustration. We are constantly reminding our friends in South America of this fact of life, and we cannot consistently disregard it in our own affairs.

Egalitarianism may also be necessary for a viable economy. The Keynesian school of economists so argues, and while the relation between distribution, saving, consumption, and investment is far from an agreed matter, one can give some credence to the view that a relatively even distribution is conducive to growth, stability, and full employment. Again, we do not hesitate to tell Latin America that what it needs for industrialization is a better internal market.

Egalitarianism fosters human resources, which are the molecules with which all our economic and social institutions are built. This bids fair to become the greatest discovery of the twentieth century.

Some economists, notably the so-called welfare economists, will deplore the fact that we cannot measure any of the above nor prove its truth beyond a reasonable difference of opinion. So what? Computers are useful in assembling collateral evidence, but we have not reached nor should seek to reach the day when the voter can abdicate in their favor.

Egalitarianism may be promoted in many ways, but one is permitted to hope that it will get some assistance from the tax system.

The theory of progressive taxation got off to a bad start with John Stuart Mill, who introduced the idea that equality in taxation is a matter of hedonistic sacrifice; later it became engulfed in a maze of marginal utility doctrine. It says that the rich should pay more than the poor up to the point where psychic pain is equalized (or minimized). This precipitated a long and futile search for a rule to measure psychic pain. Moreover, one suspects that psychic pain from taxes is not entirely a matter of economic status; Republicans seem more susceptible to it than democrats. Economists have hesitated to tread over their boundary lines into political science, where a much more significant analysis could be made in terms of the distribution of political power and the effects of economic status on political viability and stability.

Or staying within their field, economists might argue the matter in terms of social costs. All private income has social significance in terms of the amenities it makes possible and their effect on people. Naturally, this effect is greatest at the bottom of the income scale. Viewed in this light, progressive taxation is but a case of reducing the (social) opportunity cost of public expenditures.

All of the above, of course, involves the matter of degree, which can never be more certain or precise than the principle of progression itself. And as we have argued (Blum and Kalven notwithstanding), even proportional taxation involves the same kind, if not the same degree, of value judgments. There is no natural order of tax distribution.

It can be argued plausibly that, with due regard for the political realities, the price we now pay for a high degree of formal progression is too high. The price is in terms of horizontal equities, or in layman's terms, the loopholes which subvert the progressive scale in many cases. The argument assumes that some of the formal progression in the income tax scale could be traded for more uniform application. We shall consider this later.

Special Privilege and Qualitative Taxation

The reviewer lends a responsive ear to those who deplore the fact that our tax system leans so heavily on quantitative measures and offers so little in qualitative distinctions among the sources of income and wealth. If it be true that there is much reaping without sowing in our system of distribution or that some output is secure in terms of incentive and some is highly susceptible to repression, and if a main purpose of economic strategy in general and tax strategy in particular is to foster growth in the wealth of nations, then differentiation and discrimination in the selection of tax bases would seem worthy of top attention. The trouble here lies in our facilities of discernment. John A. Hobson appeared to have found the high road toward prescribing a tax system based on qualitative distinctions, but in the end he surrendered to a quantitative measure. Henry George and John R. Commons concentrated on one element in economic rewards that seemed to them especially strategic for taxation, namely, the rent of land. Even this most definitive surplus contains impurities which Commons sought to exclude.

The reviewer accepts the interpretation that there is a substantial core of truth in the counsel of these differentiators. It should have more appeal for those who worry most about the effects of taxes on incentives.

A discriminating tax system, concerned about incentives, would surely give more emphasis to death taxes than our system does. Estate and gift taxes are the area of the tax system which suffers from greatest neglect. The resulting product is not only weak in yield, but it is capricious in incidence and a trap for the unwary. Detail is out of place here, but we may suggest as reforms worthy of consideration the exemption of transfers to spouses, pooling of transfers by spouses to others, integration of gift and death transfers, and better account of the time-lapse between transfers.

Experimentation with a graded property tax, probably confined to urban areas, deserves more interest and support than it has attracted. The element of truth and wisdom in land-taxation proposals needs revived interest, if only as a defense of local property taxes as against sales taxes and as a challenge of favoritism for natural resources and capital gains in the income tax.

But when this is said, we must conclude that qualitative differentiation in taxation has not won and probably will not win many battles. It is clear enough that in our day of oligopolistic industry and sporadic competition, unearned income must be a ubiquitous phenomenon. Hobson followed a sound intuition in seeking to isolate these gains for taxation, but he did not succeed in developing a method.

Harmony and Discord in Taxation

The institutional economists observed that in their day, in contrast to the one in which much economic doctrine was concocted, decisions were the product of collective action. Whereas the older economists had sought to find a harmony of interests, the institutionalists were resigned to much conflict held within some bounds by the balance of power, compromise agreements, and working rules, some of which were sanctioned in the last instance by the Supreme Court.

The conflict of interests is surely no stranger to the field of taxation. This nation was born in tax conflict. The thought then was that democratic procedure might remove this curse from the levy. The issue was fought to a successful conclusion, but enough of the curse remained to punctuate our history with a whiskey rebellion, a near-secession, one of the stormiest decisions of the Supreme Court, and other lesser events.

But public finance is not all conflict, and one can also observe many harmonies among the discords. The one harmony stressed by Roy Blough in a discerning essay on the subject[1] is the common interest in more productivity— economic growth. When two dogs are quarreling about a bone, the uncontroversial solution is to find another bone and give each one. Perhaps this was the motif that captured so much unity of support for the Revenue Act of 1964. Surely this was an impressive phenomenon: the AFL-CIO supported the bill; the U.S. Chamber of Commerce supported it; many industrial associations supported it; and intellectuals more than 400 strong from top-notch universities and colleges supported it. One could tell his seminar to look closely at this situation because they might never see its like again.

Fortunately, some egalitarianism, if not for its own sake, then for its by-

1. Roy Blough, "Conflict and Harmony in Taxation" (An address before the American Philosophic Society, February 18, 1944); published in part in Harold M. Groves, *Viewpoints on Public Finance* (New York: Henry Holt and Co., 1947), pp. 712-20.

product, can be supported plausibly by all classes of society. The rich may support progressive taxation not only because the marginal dollars they pay for public services are perhaps worth less subjectively to them than to the poor, not only because they may prefer philanthropies that require a like contribution from others of their own station, but also because the rich are as much involved as the rest of us in such by-products of reduced inequality as political stability, economic growth, and especially, the conservation and improvement of human resources on which a healthy society depends.

When interests conflict they can sometimes be compromised. We have seldom, if ever, tried to apply the institution of collective bargaining to taxation. But a tax study (bargaining) committee representing the various interest groups might be worth trying. If the AFL-CIO and the U.S. Chamber of Commerce could agree on a program, Congress just conceivably might react as it did last time: "What therefore God has joined together, let no man put asunder."

Is there any give and take which might provide the basis for such a compromise and which could improve the tax system? There is, or at least there might be, in a context of reduced military spending. For example, labor might yield further ground on both income tax rates and the nominal degree of progression. It might be persuaded, as previously noted, that the price we pay (in terms of horizontal equity) for much formal progression is too high. The Chamber might yield ground on capital gains and percentage depletion and death tax anomalies. Both might accept a moderate broad-based tax—preferably on adjusted gross income with moderate minimal exemptions—in lieu of a lot of indefensible excises and part of our social security tax system. Our social security payroll taxes may be regarded as a tax on employment. At the present 11 or 12 percent rate in an era when unemployment is a major problem they must impress many people as anomalous. Thrown into the package, too, might be more relief for the states where needs are most pressing and taxes most regressive. The above is not presented as a tax program but rather as an example of how conflicting interests could unite to improve the tax system.

Not that anyone need be too sanguine about the success of this program. Notwithstanding formidable support, the 1964 tax bill lost many of its reform features along the road to passage. Congress is understandably jealous of its tax-making function and it is not likely to take kindly to the suggestion that it abdicate its powers in favor of an ad hoc legislature. There are many people to whom the very idea of compromise is abhorrent and evil. But our tax system is not so good that we should pass up lightly any procedural experiment that has a bare chance of success.

Value Judgments

We have suggested that almost all the vital questions in public finance require judgment and evaluation for an answer. And we have added the view that they are not less worth study and review on that account. This book has been an attempt to help the reader make an evaluation of his own. The public interest may be a nebulous thing, but in a democracy the search for it is inevitable and never-ending.

Index

Index

Index

COMPOSED BY HORNE ASSOCIATES, INC., HANOVER, NEW HAMPSHIRE
MANUFACTURED BY MALLOY LITHOGRAPHING, INC., ANN ARBOR, MICHIGAN
TEXT LINES ARE SET IN PRESS ROMAN, DISPLAY LINES IN TIMES ROMAN

Library of Congress Cataloging in Publication Data
Groves, Harold Martin, 1897–1969.
Tax philosophers.
Includes bibliographical references.
1. Taxation–Great Britain–History.
2. Taxation–United States–History. I. Curran,
Donald J., 1926–   ed. II. Title.
HJ2317.G76   336.2'00942   74-5901
ISBN 0-299-06660-6